JET TILA'S

ONE PAN FOUR SEASONS

CREDITS

1610 N. 2nd St., Suite 102, Milwaukee WI 53212-3906

International Standard Book Number:
978-1-61765-979-9

Cover photography: Trusted Studios
Jet Tila portrait: Matt Wagemann

Pictured on front cover:
Spring: Asparagus & Shrimp with Angel Hair, p. 37
Summer: Spicy Chicken Fajitas, p. 89
Fall: Caramel-Apple Skillet Buckle, p. 166
Winter: Deep-Dish Sausage Pizza, p. 193

Pictured on back cover:
Spring: Strawberry Buttermilk Shortcake, p. 65
Summer: Salmon with Mango-Citrus Salsa, p. 97
Fall: Maple & Bacon Glazed Sprouts, p. 153
Winter: Savory Breakfast Casserole, p. 174

Printed in the USA
1 3 5 7 9 10 8 6 4 2

Herbed Noodles with Edamame, p. 53

CONTENTS

SPRING

BREAKFAST

SMALL PLATES

MAIN COURSES

SIDES

DESSERTS

SUMMER

BREAKFAST

SMALL PLATES

MAIN COURSES

SIDES

DESSERTS

Fried Green Tomato Napoleons with Slaw, p. 85

FALL

BREAKFAST

SMALL PLATES

MAIN COURSES

Garlic Potatoes & Peppers, p. 154

WINTER

ONE PAN TO RULE THEM ALL

Trust me. I know how busy life gets. As a chef devoted to my family and career, I'm always looking for ways to squeeze more into my day. It's one of the reasons I'm so excited to have worked with Copper Chef on the Titan Pan. The do-it-all skillet combines the pro-chef power of stainless steel and aluminum with the utility of a nonstick surface, making both cooking and cleanup easy. You'll be amazed at how quickly the pan heats. In no time, you can achieve the perfect sizzle and then watch food slide right off the surface when you serve it. And believe me when I say you can use it to cook almost anything.

If your kids are like mine, they love comfort foods. Pasta. Chicken strips. Pizza. Burgers. You can cook them all in the Titan Pan. Got carnivores in your household? Searing large pieces of meat like steaks, fish and chicken can be difficult on the stove. With the Titan Pan, you can get your sear and then finish the dish in the oven for even cooking. And for those especially crazy days, you can simplify mealtime by doing all your cooking in one pan.

On the Tila homefront, we're breakfast lovers. So we start our bacon in the Titan Pan, then fry eggs and make pancakes in it, too. You can cook any meal for the entire family all in one pan.

Home cooks and restaurant chefs alike are always on the hunt for recipes that use fresh fruits and veggies as central ingredients. That's where this companion cookbook comes into play. Created exclusively for use with the Titan Pan, it organizes tasty meals, side dishes, appetizers and desserts by the flavors and ingredients that are quintessentially spring, summer, fall and winter. Of course, you can enjoy the recipes any time of year. And you can always swap fresh ingredients for frozen or even canned ones if that is what's easiest to get your hands on. The goal, after all, is to make cooking for family and friends practical and fun. And to make each and every mealtime memorable.

So enjoy *One Pan, Four Seasons*. And happy cooking in your Titan Pan!

COPPER CHEF
TITAN SERIES

TITAN PAN QUICK GUIDE

This technological marvel will become your go-to for its ability to make almost any recipe — on the stovetop and in the oven.

12 PANS IN ONE Fryer. Wok. Steamer. Pizza pan. Baking dish. These are just some of the Titan Pan's functions. The recipes in this cookbook allow you to take advantage of all of them. We've given tips along the way so you can use it with ease for years to come.

DEEP OPPORTUNITIES The Titan Pan holds 4 quarts (16 cups), making it the perfect alternative to a Dutch oven. Use it to cook cozy soups and stews like the Tuscan Portobello Stew on page 200.

COOK & LOOK Heat resistant to 350°, the Titan Pan's clear lid lets you see how your food is coming along without having to repeatedly lift the lid.

MIX & SERVE Super resistant to scratching, the Titan Pan will let you use a hand mixer with no worries—and you can also confidently remove portions of food from the pan with metal serving utensils.

NONSTICK TIP Avoid using nonstick cooking sprays in the Titan Pan. These products can leave a sticky residue that builds up over time, impairing the nonstick surface. Instead, use butter, or, when baking, use a pastry or basting brush to coat the pan with a thin layer of shortening.

GRIP IT If you like thick oven gloves and hot pads, you'll appreciate the wide handles on the pan and lid, which allow for easy maneuvering of dishes like Deep-Dish Sausage Pizza, on page 192, in and out of the oven.

OVEN SMARTS Because the handle causes the Titan Pan to sit slightly off-center in the oven, it's a good idea to rotate the pan halfway through the cook time for even heating.

CLEANING CARE The Titan Pan is dishwasher-safe, but hand-washing it after every use is the best way to care for the product.

THE WELL-STOCKED KITCHEN

Every kitchen needs key staples on hand. With this list of foods and gear, you can whip up all the recipes in this cookbook — and other family favorites.

FOOD STAPLES

Absolute must-stocks on any pantry list are salt, pepper, all-purpose flour, sugar and soy sauce. Also, count on fresh herbs like thyme, rosemary and basil (turn the page to Season's Best for more). For dry herbs and spices, keep cumin, cinnamon and chili powder at the ready. To speed up the preparation of all your meals, snacks and even desserts, these additional ingredients are also smart to have around.

QUICK-COOKING MEATS such as boneless chicken, pork tenderloin, pork chops and ground meat make for easy meals. Don't forget sausage, sirloin flank steaks, fish and shrimp. They cook up fast as well.

PASTAS AND RICE MIXES are pantry staples that have a long shelf life and complement a multitude of entrees.

CONDIMENTS, including ketchup, mustard, mayonnaise, salad dressings, salsa, taco sauce, soy sauce and lemon juice, add flavor without much work.

FRESH PRODUCE in the fridge leads to quick side dishes as well as healthy snacks. Ready-to-use salad greens are a modern cook's friend.

DRIED HERBS, SPICES, VINEGARS AND SEASONING MIXES add instant flavor, keep for months and help you prepare an endless number of dishes.

PASTA SAUCES, OLIVES, BEANS, BROTHS AND CANNED TOMATOES are ideal to have on hand for numerous recipes. They can be a no-brainer base of a quick meal.

KITCHEN TOOLS & GADGETS

Having the right cooking gear on hand makes every kitchen task easier. Make sure your pantry is equipped with these go-to basics.

- Apple corer
- Blender and/or food processor
- Can and bottle opener
- Citrus juicer
- Citrus zester
- Colander
- Cookie cutters
- Corkscrew
- Wooden cutting boards
- Dough cutter/ scraper
- Egg separator
- Egg slicer
- Garlic press
- Hand grater/ shredder
- Ladles, large and small
- Measuring cups, dry and liquid
- Measuring spoons
- Meat fork
- Meat mallet/ tenderizer
- Metal skewers
- Metal strainer or sieve
- Mixing bowls
- Pancake turners
- Pastry bag and tips
- Pastry blender
- Pastry brush
- Pepper mill
- Pie server
- Pizza cutter
- Plastic mixing spoons
- Potato masher
- Rolling pin
- Slotted spoons, large and small
- Spatulas, rubber and metal
- Stand mixer
- Storage freezer containers
- Thermometers: instant read, candy/deep-fry, meat, oven, refrigerator/ freezer
- Timer
- Tongs
- Vegetable peeler
- Wire cooking racks
- Wire whisks in assorted sizes
- Wooden mixing spoons

KITCHEN CUTLERY

A basic set of knives is essential. Why? There are a variety of knives made from numerous materials, and each has a unique task. The best knives, made from high-carbon steel, are resistant to corrosion (unlike carbon steel) and remain sharper longer than stainless steel.

UTILITY KNIFE This 6-in. knife is the right size to slice small foods.

CARVING KNIFE This 8- to 10-in. knife is perfect for slicing roasts and turkey.

CHEF'S KNIFE This multipurpose knife with an 8- to 10-in. blade is used for mincing, chopping and dicing.

PARING KNIFE This 3- to 4-in. knife is used for peeling, mincing and slicing small foods.

BONING KNIFE This knife's 5- or 6-in. tapered blade is designed to remove the meat from poultry, beef, pork or fish bones.

KITCHEN SHEARS This versatile tool is used to snip fresh herbs, disjoint chicken, trim pastry, cut kitchen string and perform many other tasks.

STEEL This long, thin rod with a handle is used to smooth out small rough spots on the edge of a knife blade and to reset the edge of the blade. You can also use a whetstone or electric knife sharpener to sharpen knives.

SERRATED Sawlike teeth catch and slice through food such as bread, tomatoes, grapes, heads of lettuce and eggplants, and the knife is equally good on melons, chocolate and even roast beef. It's a kitchen workhorse.

KNOW YOUR FRESH PRODUCE & HERBS

While it's ideal to cook with fresh fruits and veggies, we're fortunate to have a multitude of options in both the frozen- and canned-foods aisles of our grocery stores. This enables us to cook our favorite dishes any time of year — no matter if a particular item of produce is in peak season. Still, if you want to maximize flavor and freshness, here's some advice on what to look for throughout the year.

FARM-FRESH PICKIN'S

Sure, you can find most fruits and vegetables in grocery stores year-round. But to include the freshest ingredients in your recipes, timing is everything. Here's what's best to buy according to season.

SPRING

Artichokes
Asparagus
Arugula
Avocados
Butter lettuce
Chard
Green beans
Mango
Morel mushrooms
Parsnips
Radishes
Rhubarb
Snap peas
Spinach

SUMMER

Apricots
Baby carrots
Cherries
Cucumbers
Bell peppers
Blueberries
Boysenberries
Cantaloupe
Corn
Eggplant
Figs
Green beans
Hearts of palm
Key limes
Lima beans
Long beans
Melon
Okra
Onions
Peaches
Pineapple
Raspberries
Snap peas
Snow peas
Tomatoes
Watermelon
Zucchini

FALL

Acorn squash
Apples
Beets
Broccoli
Cauliflower
Celery
Cranberries
Endive
Garlic
Ginger
Grapes
Jalepeno peppers
Kohlrabi
Mushrooms
Pears
Potatoes
Pumpkin
Quince
Sweet potatoes

WINTER

Brussels sprouts
Cabbage
Dates
Grapefruit
Horseradish
Kale
Mandarin oranges
Passion fruit
Radicchio
Tangerines
Turnips
Winter squash

4 MUST-HAVE FLAVORS

Get to know these classic herbs better—and then get creative with them in the kitchen.

1. BASIL

Flavor: You may pick up hints of pepper, anise and mint.

How to use it: Pair it with mild cheeses, fresh tomatoes and spicy flavors. It's most commonly used in Mediterranean, Asian and Indian dishes. For maximum flavor and to prevent browning, add it at the end of cooking.

Slicing: Remove the leaves and discard the stems, as the leaves hold the most flavor. Stack leaves, then roll up. Slice through the roll to make thin strips.

2. CILANTRO (AKA CORIANDER LEAF)

Flavor: To some, it's bright and lemon-zesty. To others, it's "soapy," perhaps because of its genetic makeup.

How to use it: Like most herbs, cilantro can be eaten raw or cooked, and it brings the dullest sauces to life with its invigorating flavor profile. It's a staple in Latin American and Asian cooking.

Chopping: Hold the bunch, then angle the blade of a chef's knife almost parallel with the stems. With short, downward strokes, shave off leaves where they meet the stems. Chop as recipe directs.

3. THYME

Flavor: Thyme is a pungent herb with a slightly sweet and woodsy flavor. The leaves are aromatic and floral and have a strong yet understated taste.

How to use it: A staple in French cooking and a key ingredient in herbes de Provence, thyme works well with poultry (think chicken salad). You can use it in breads, desserts and cocktails, and it pairs well with strong cheeses. For best results, strip leaves from stems and chop before use.

Prepping: Grab the stem with one hand and use your other hand to pull the leaves down the stem. Don't worry if you get small bits of stem in the herb pile.

4. DILL

Flavor: Delicate strands boast a strong flavor of clean, fresh earthiness or a subtle licorice- or fennel-like flavor.

How to use it: Dill is best used in small quantities; too much can overwhelm a dish. It works well in spring salads, pairs nicely with vegetables like asparagus and peas, and is a tasty addition to homemade salad dressings. The tangy herb is commonly associated with German and Scandinavian cooking.

Chopping: Pull the feathery fronds from stems and discard stems. Coarsely chop the fronds, but keep in mind, the more you chop, the stronger the flavor.

CHAPTER 1

SPRING

ALMOND BERRY PANCAKES

SERVES 5

PREP: 15 MIN. COOK: 5 MIN./BATCH

- ¾ cup all-purpose flour
- ½ cup whole wheat flour
- ¼ cup sugar
- 2 tsp. baking powder
- Dash salt
- 1 large egg, room temperature, lightly beaten
- 1¼ cups fat-free milk
- 2 Tbsp. butter, melted
- ½ tsp. almond extract
- ½ cup fresh raspberries
- ½ cup fresh blueberries
- Optional: Confectioners' sugar and additional fresh berries

In a large bowl, combine the flours, sugar, baking powder and salt. In a small bowl, combine the egg, milk, butter and extract; stir into dry ingredients just until moistened.

Pour batter by ¼ cupfuls into a lightly greased Titan Pan; sprinkle with berries. Turn when bubbles form on top. Cook until the second side is golden brown. Garnish with confectioners' sugar and additional berries if desired.

2 PANCAKES *239 cal., 6g fat (3g sat. fat), 56mg chol., 262mg sod., 40g carb. (16g sugars, 3g fiber), 7g pro.*

"Get all your prep work done and organized before cooking. If everything is organized and ready, you limit the mistakes you can make."

PISTACHIO GRANOLA

SERVES 12

PREP: 10 MIN. COOK: 15 MIN. + COOLING

- 2 cups old-fashioned oats
- ⅔ cup packed brown sugar
- ¼ cup apple cider or unsweetened apple juice
- ½ tsp. ground cinnamon
- ¼ tsp. salt
- ⅔ cup Cheerios
- ⅔ cup pistachios, chopped
- ⅔ cup dried cherries
- ½ cup dried apples, chopped
- ½ cup dried blueberries
- ½ cup sunflower kernels

In the Titan Pan, toast oats over medium heat until golden brown. Remove and set aside. In the same pan, cook and stir brown sugar and apple cider over medium-low heat until brown sugar is dissolved, 1-2 minutes. Add cinnamon and salt; stir to combine.

Stir in the cereal, pistachios, dried fruits, sunflower kernels and toasted oats until coated. Cool. Store in an airtight container.

½ CUP *233 cal., 7g fat (1g sat. fat), 0 chol., 122mg sod., 39g carb. (22g sugars, 4g fiber), 5g pro.*

BANANA-HAZELNUT FRENCH TOAST

SERVES 4
TAKES: 30 MIN.

- 8 slices French bread (½ in. thick)
- ¼ cup cream cheese, softened
- ¼ cup Nutella®
- 1 medium banana, halved lengthwise and sliced
- 4 tsp. brown sugar
- 4 large eggs
- 1 cup 2% milk
- ¼ cup hazelnut liqueur
- 2 tsp. ground cinnamon
- 2 tsp. vanilla extract
- 2 Tbsp. butter
- Optional toppings: Confectioners' sugar, maple syrup, fresh mint leaves, additional banana slices and additional Nutella®

On each of 4 bread slices, spread cream cheese and Nutella® to within ½ in. of edges. Top with banana slices, brown sugar and remaining bread. In a shallow bowl, whisk eggs, milk, liqueur, cinnamon and vanilla.

In the Titan Pan, heat butter over medium-low heat. Dip both sides of sandwiches in egg mixture, allowing each side to soak 30 seconds. Place sandwiches in skillet; toast until golden brown, 4-5 minutes on each side. Top as desired.

1 STUFFED FRENCH TOAST *469 cal., 23g fat (10g sat. fat), 221mg chol., 340mg sod., 48g carb. (29g sugars, 3g fiber), 13g pro.*

HEALTH
TIP

Use any type of hearty whole grain bread, cut to size if needed, instead of French bread to increase fiber.

ITALIAN CLOUD EGGS

SERVES 4
TAKES: 25 MIN.

- 4 large eggs, separated
- ¼ tsp. Italian seasoning
- ⅛ tsp. salt
- ⅛ tsp. pepper
- ¼ cup shredded Parmesan cheese
- 1 Tbsp. minced fresh basil
- 1 Tbsp. finely chopped oil-packed sun-dried tomatoes

Preheat oven to 450°. Separate eggs; place whites in a large bowl and the yolks in 4 separate small bowls. Beat egg whites, Italian seasoning, salt and pepper until stiff peaks form.

In a lightly greased Titan Pan, drop the egg white mixture into 4 mounds. With the back of a spoon, create a small well in the center of each mound. Sprinkle with cheese. Bake until light brown, about 5 minutes. Gently slip an egg yolk into each of the mounds. Bake until yolks are set, 3-5 minutes longer. Sprinkle with basil and tomatoes. Serve immediately.

1 SERVING *96 cal., 6g fat (2g sat. fat), 190mg chol., 234mg sod., 1g carb. (0 sugars, 0 fiber), 8g pro.*

GET CRACKIN'

If you want to advance your culinary skills and use simple physics to impress your friends and family, crack one egg by hitting it against another. The magic? The second egg won't break. **Here's the trick:** Hold an egg in each hand. Tap the eggs together (at the equator, where it's easiest to break the egg). One egg will be cracked; the other won't. Use your fingers to split open the eggshell, then pour the yolk and white out into a bowl. Once you've cracked all the eggs but one, crack the final egg against the countertop.

LEMON TORTILLA FRENCH TOAST

SERVES 6

PREP: 25 MIN. COOK: 5 MIN./BATCH

- 1 pkg. (8 oz.) cream cheese, softened
- 6 Tbsp. lemon curd, divided
- 2 tsp. grated lemon zest
- ⅛ tsp. almond extract
- 2 large eggs
- 2 Tbsp. heavy whipping cream
- 1 Tbsp. poppy seeds
- 3 Tbsp. butter
- 6 flour tortillas (6 in.)
- 1⅓ cups fresh blackberries
- ¼ cup seedless blackberry spreadable fruit
- Additional grated lemon zest, optional

In a small bowl, beat cream cheese, 3 Tbsp. lemon curd, lemon zest and extract until fluffy. Set aside.

In a shallow bowl, whisk eggs, cream and remaining 3 Tbsp. lemon curd until blended; stir in poppy seeds. In the Titan Pan, heat 1 Tbsp. butter over medium heat. Dip both sides of a tortilla in egg mixture, allowing excess to drip off. Place in pan; toast until golden brown, 2-3 minutes on each side. Remove to a wire rack. Repeat with remaining tortillas, adding butter to the pan as needed.

Spread about 3 Tbsp. cream cheese mixture over each tortilla to within ¼ in. of edges. Fold tortillas in half over filling. In a microwave-safe bowl, combine the blackberries and spreadable fruit; microwave, covered, at 50% power until warmed, 2-3 minutes, stirring once. Serve with tortillas and, if desired, additional grated lemon zest.

1 FILLED TORTILLA *445 cal., 27g fat (15g sat. fat), 134mg chol., 403mg sod., 42g carb. (21g sugars, 3g fiber), 8g pro.*

HEALTH TIP

Use whole wheat tortillas and get almost twice the fiber per serving.

CURRY CARROT DIP

SERVES 8
TAKES: 30 MIN.

- 1 small onion, chopped
- 2 tsp. canola oil
- 4 medium carrots, sliced
- ⅓ cup water
- ¼ tsp. salt
- ¼ tsp. pepper
- ¼ tsp. curry powder
- 2 Tbsp. reduced-fat mayonnaise
- 2 tsp. prepared mustard
- Assorted raw vegetables

In the Titan Pan, saute onion in oil. Add carrots, water, salt, pepper and curry. Bring to a boil. Reduce heat; cover and simmer for 6 minutes or until the vegetables are tender. Uncover; cook for 8 minutes or until liquid has evaporated. Cool.

Transfer to a food processor or blender; cover and process until smooth. Add mayonnaise and mustard; mix well. Serve with vegetables.

2 TBSP. *40 cal., 3g fat (0 sat. fat), 1mg chol., 133mg sod., 4g carb. (2g sugars, 1g fiber), 0 pro.*

HEALTH
TIP

Don't peel the carrots—the skin contains lots of nutrients. But do scrub them well before chopping.

CRAWFISH BEIGNETS WITH FIERY DIP

CRAWFISH BEIGNETS WITH FIERY DIP

SERVES 24

PREP: 20 MIN. COOK: 5 MIN./BATCH

- 1 large egg, beaten
- 1 lb. chopped cooked crawfish tail meat or shrimp
- 4 green onions, chopped
- 1½ tsp. butter, melted
- ½ tsp. salt
- ½ tsp. cayenne pepper
- ⅓ cup bread flour
- Oil for deep-fat frying
- ¾ cup mayonnaise
- ½ cup ketchup
- ¼ tsp. prepared horseradish, optional
- ¼ tsp. hot pepper sauce

In a large bowl, combine the egg, crawfish, onions, butter, salt and cayenne. Stir in flour until blended.

In the Titan Pan, heat 1 in. oil to 375°. Drop batter by tablespoonfuls, a few at a time, into hot oil. Fry until golden brown on both sides. Drain on paper towels.

In a small bowl, combine the mayonnaise, ketchup, horseradish if desired, and hot pepper sauce. Serve with beignets.

1 BEIGNET WITH 1½ TSP. SAUCE *101 cal., 8g fat (1g sat. fat), 35mg chol., 171mg sod., 3g carb. (1g sugars, 0 fiber), 4g pro.*

"Switch to kosher salt as your primary salt. The more you season with it, the more you realize food needs more salt than you think."

SHRIMP CORN CAKES WITH SOY MAYO

SERVES 24

PREP: 30 MIN. COOK: 5 MIN./BATCH

- ½ cup mayonnaise
- 1 Tbsp. reduced-sodium soy sauce
- 1 Tbsp. ketchup
- 2 tsp. Dijon mustard
- ½ tsp. garlic powder
- ½ tsp. hot pepper sauce, optional
- ⅛ tsp. pepper

SHRIMP CORN CAKES

- ½ cup chopped onion (about 1 small)
- 1 Tbsp. oil plus additional for frying, divided
- 2 garlic cloves, minced
- ½ lb. uncooked peeled and deveined shrimp, finely chopped
- ¾ cup all-purpose flour
- ¼ cup cornmeal
- 1 Tbsp. cornstarch
- 1 tsp. baking powder
- ¼ tsp. salt
- ¼ tsp. pepper
- 1 cup cream-style corn
- 1 cup whole kernel corn
- 1 large egg, lightly beaten

In a small bowl, combine the first 7 ingredients. Cover and chill until serving.

In the Titan Pan, cook and stir the onion in 1 Tbsp. oil over medium-high heat until tender. Add garlic; cook 1 minute longer. Add shrimp; cook and stir until shrimp turns pink. Remove from the heat.

In a large bowl, mix the flour, cornmeal, cornstarch, baking powder, salt and pepper. In a small bowl, mix corn, egg and the shrimp mixture; stir into the dry ingredients just until moistened.

Wipe pan clean; heat ¼ in. of oil to 375°. In batches, drop corn mixture by rounded tablespoonfuls into oil; fry until golden brown, 1½ minutes on each side. Drain on paper towels. Serve with sauce.

1 CORN CAKE WITH 1 TSP. SAUCE *109 cal., 7g fat (1g sat. fat), 22mg chol., 183mg sod., 8g carb. (1g sugars, 1g fiber), 3g pro.*

CHINESE SCALLION PANCAKES

SERVES 8
PREP: 35 MIN + STANDING COOK: 5 MIN./BATCH

- 3 cups all-purpose flour
- 1⅓ cups boiling water
- 4 tsp. sesame oil
- 6 green onions, chopped
- 1 tsp. salt
- ½ cup canola oil

DIPPING SAUCE

- 3 Tbsp. reduced-sodium soy sauce
- 1 Tbsp. brown sugar
- 2 tsp. minced fresh gingerroot
- 2 tsp. rice vinegar
- ½ tsp. sesame oil
- ⅛ tsp. crushed red pepper flakes

Place flour in a large bowl; stir in boiling water until dough forms a ball. Turn onto a floured surface; knead until smooth and elastic, 4-6 minutes. Place in a large bowl; cover and let rest for 30 minutes.

Divide dough into 8 portions; roll each portion into an 8-in. circle. Brush each with ½ tsp. sesame oil; sprinkle with 1 heaping Tbsp. green onion and ⅛ tsp. salt. Roll up jelly-roll style; holding an end of a rope, wrap the dough around, forming a coil, pinching to seal. Flatten slightly. Roll each coil to ⅛-in. thickness.

In the Titan Pan, heat 1 Tbsp. canola oil. Over medium-high heat, cook 1 pancake at a time until golden brown, 2-3 minutes on each side, adding oil as needed.

Meanwhile, in a small bowl, combine the sauce ingredients. Serve with pancakes.

1 PANCAKE WITH 1½ TSP. SAUCE *333 cal., 17g fat (1g sat. fat), 0 chol., 534mg sod., 39g carb. (2g sugars, 2g fiber), 5g pro.*

GINGER PORK LETTUCE WRAPS

SERVES 24
TAKES: 30 MIN.

- 1 lb. lean ground pork
- 1 medium onion, chopped
- ¼ cup hoisin sauce
- 4 garlic cloves, minced
- 1 Tbsp. minced fresh gingerroot
- 1 Tbsp. red wine vinegar
- 1 Tbsp. reduced-sodium soy sauce
- 2 tsp. Thai chili sauce
- 1 can (8 oz.) sliced water chestnuts, drained and finely chopped
- 4 green onions, chopped
- 1 Tbsp. sesame oil
- 24 Bibb or Boston lettuce leaves

In the Titan Pan, cook pork and onion over medium heat 6-8 minutes or until pork is no longer pink and onion is tender, breaking up pork into crumbles.

Stir in hoisin sauce, garlic, ginger, vinegar, soy sauce and chili sauce until blended. Add water chestnuts, green onions and sesame oil; heat through. To serve, place pork mixture in lettuce leaves; fold lettuce over filling.

Freeze option Freeze cooled meat mixture in freezer containers. To use, partially thaw in refrigerator overnight. Heat through in a saucepan, stirring occasionally; add a little water if necessary.

1 FILLED LETTUCE WRAP *54 cal., 3g fat (1g sat. fat), 11mg chol., 87mg sod., 4g carb. (2g sugars, 1g fiber), 4g pro.*

CHEF TIP

Use the edge of a spoon to peel the ginger.

GINGER PORK LETTUCE WRAPS

ASPARAGUS & SHRIMP WITH ANGEL HAIR

SERVES 2
TAKES: 30 MIN.

- 3 oz. uncooked angel hair pasta
- ½ lb. uncooked shrimp (16-20 per lb.), peeled and deveined
- ¼ tsp. salt
- ⅛ tsp. crushed red pepper flakes
- 2 Tbsp. olive oil, divided
- 8 fresh asparagus spears, trimmed and cut into 2-in. pieces
- ½ cup sliced fresh mushrooms
- ¼ cup chopped seeded tomato, peeled
- 4 garlic cloves, minced
- 2 tsp. chopped green onion
- ½ cup white wine or chicken broth
- 1½ tsp. minced fresh basil
- 1½ tsp. minced fresh oregano
- 1½ tsp. minced fresh parsley
- 1½ tsp. minced fresh thyme
- ¼ cup grated Parmesan cheese
- Lemon wedges

Cook pasta in the Titan Pan according to package directions. Drain and set aside, keeping warm.

Sprinkle shrimp with salt and red pepper flakes. In the Titan Pan, heat 1 Tbsp. oil over medium-high heat. Add shrimp; stir-fry until pink, 2-3 minutes. Remove; keep warm. In same pan, stir-fry the next 5 ingredients in the remaining oil until vegetables are crisp-tender, about 5 minutes. Add wine and seasonings. Return shrimp to pan.

Add pasta to shrimp mixture and toss gently. Cook and stir until heated through, 1-2 minutes. Sprinkle with Parmesan cheese. Serve with lemon wedges.

1¾ CUPS *488 cal., 19g fat (4g sat. fat), 132mg chol., 584mg sod., 41g carb. (4g sugars, 3g fiber), 29g pro.*

SOUTHERN FRIED CHICKEN WITH GRAVY

SERVES 6

PREP: 25 MIN. COOK: 45 MIN.

- 1 cup all-purpose flour
- 1 tsp. onion powder
- 1 tsp. paprika
- ¾ tsp. salt
- ½ tsp. rubbed sage
- ½ tsp. pepper
- ¼ tsp. dried thyme
- 1 large egg
- ½ cup whole milk
- 1 broiler/fryer chicken (3 to 3½ lbs.), cut up
- Oil for frying

CREAMY GRAVY

- ⅓ cup all-purpose flour
- ¼ tsp. salt
- ¼ tsp. dried thyme
- ¼ to ½ tsp. pepper
- 2½ cups whole milk
- ½ cup heavy whipping cream

In a shallow dish, combine the first 7 ingredients. In a shallow bowl, beat egg and milk. Dip chicken pieces into egg mixture, then place in flour mixture, a few pieces at a time, and turn to coat.

In the Titan Pan, heat ¼ in. of oil; fry chicken until browned on all sides. Cook, covered, until juices run clear and chicken is tender, 35-40 minutes, turning occasionally. Uncover and cook 5 minutes longer. Drain on paper towels and keep warm. Drain pan, reserving 3 Tbsp. drippings in pan.

For gravy, in a small bowl, combine the flour, salt, thyme and pepper. Gradually whisk in milk and cream until smooth; add to pan. Bring to a boil over medium heat; cook and stir for 2 minutes or until thickened. Serve with chicken.

5 OZ. COOKED CHICKEN: *750 cal., 52g fat (14g sat. fat), 170mg chol., 554mg sod., 28g carb. (7g sugars, 1g fiber), 41g pro.*

CHEF TIP

Before making this recipe, stir together 4 cups buttermilk, 1 Tbsp. seasoned salt and a heavy pinch of pepper in a large bowl. Submerge the chicken pieces. Turn to coat well and cover tightly. Refrigerate overnight for up to 2 days. The acidity from the buttermilk will tenderize the chicken, while the salt will penetrate the protein and give it great flavor.

SEARED SCALLOPS WITH SPINACH

SERVES 4
TAKES: 25 MIN.

- 4 bacon strips, chopped
- 12 sea scallops (about 1½ lbs.), side muscles removed
- 2 shallots, finely chopped
- ½ cup white wine or chicken broth
- 8 cups fresh baby spinach (about 8 oz.)

In the Titan Pan, cook bacon over medium heat until crisp, stirring occasionally. Remove with a slotted spoon; drain on paper towels. Discard drippings, reserving 2 Tbsp. Wipe skillet clean if necessary.

Pat scallops dry with paper towels. In same pan, heat 1 Tbsp. drippings over medium-high heat. Add the scallops; cook until golden brown and firm, 2-3 minutes on each side. Remove from the pan; keep warm.

Heat remaining drippings over medium-high heat. Add shallots; cook and stir until tender, 2-3 minutes. Add wine; bring to a boil, stirring to loosen browned bits from pan. Add the spinach; cook and stir until wilted, 1-2 minutes. Stir in bacon. Serve with scallops.

3 SCALLOPS WITH ½ CUP SPINACH MIXTURE *247 cal., 11g fat (4g sat. fat), 56mg chol., 964mg sod., 12g carb. (1g sugars, 1g fiber), 26g pro.*

CHEF TIP

Unless you live along the coasts, most scallops are frozen when they arrive at your local store. So if you're not cooking them that night, just buy scallops frozen and thaw them the day before.

SPICY CORNED BEEF TACOS

SERVES 6
TAKES: 30 MIN.

- 2 cups coleslaw mix
- 4 green onions, thinly sliced
- 2 jalapeno peppers, seeded and thinly sliced
- 1 cup Thousand Island salad dressing
- 1 to 2 Tbsp. Sriracha chili sauce
- 2 Tbsp. canola oil
- 3 cups chopped cooked corned beef
- 2 cups refrigerated diced potatoes with onion
- 12 flour tortillas (6 in.), warmed

In a small bowl, combine coleslaw mix, green onions and jalapenos. In another small bowl, whisk salad dressing and chili sauce until combined.

In the Titan Pan, heat oil over medium heat. Add corned beef and diced potatoes; cook and stir until heated through, 8-10 minutes. Serve in tortillas with coleslaw mixture and dressing mixture.

2 TACOS *621 cal., 39g fat (9g sat. fat), 60mg chol., 1606mg sod., 48g carb. (8g sugars, 4g fiber), 16g pro.*

CHEF TIP

Use a grapefruit spoon to core and seed a jalapeno pepper. The spoon's curved shape and serrated edges make it ideal for following the veggie's shape.

FILIPINO CHICKEN ADOBO

SERVES 6

PREP: 10 MIN. + MARINATING COOK: 30 MIN.

- 1 cup white vinegar
- ¼ cup soy sauce
- 1 whole garlic bulb, smashed and peeled
- 2 tsp. kosher salt
- 1 tsp. coarsely ground pepper
- 1 bay leaf
- 2 lbs. bone-in chicken thighs or drumsticks
- 1 Tbsp. canola oil
- 1 cup water

In a shallow dish, combine the first 6 ingredients. Add the chicken; refrigerate, covered, 20-30 minutes. Drain, reserving marinade. Pat chicken dry.

In the Titan Pan, heat oil over medium-high heat; brown chicken. Stir in water and reserved marinade. Bring to a boil. Reduce heat; simmer, uncovered, until the chicken is no longer pink and the sauce is slightly reduced, 20-25 minutes. Discard bay leaf. If desired, serve chicken with cooking sauce.

1 SERVING *234 cal., 15g fat (4g sat. fat), 71mg chol., 1315mg sod., 2g carb. (0 sugars, 0 fiber), 22g pro.*

GARLIC PARMESAN ASPARAGUS

SERVES 4
TAKES: 15 MIN.

- 1 lb. fresh asparagus, trimmed
- 1 garlic clove, minced
- 2 Tbsp. butter, melted
- 1 Tbsp. grated Parmesan cheese

In the Titan Pan, bring ½ in. water to a boil. Add asparagus and garlic; cook, covered, until asparagus is crisp-tender, 3-5 minutes; drain. Toss asparagus with butter and cheese.

1 SERVING *71 cal., 6g fat (4g sat. fat), 16mg chol., 74mg sod., 3g carb. (1g sugars, 1g fiber), 2g pro.*

3 WAYS TO
MINCE GARLIC

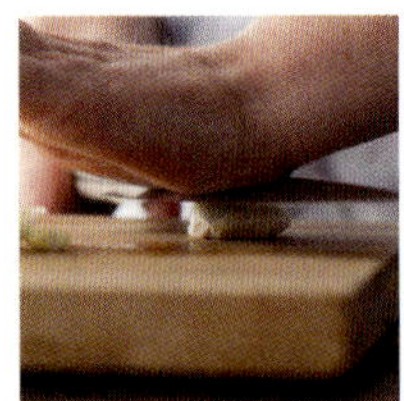

For uniform pieces, mince garlic like an onion. • Make it easy and quick by first smashing, then mincing. • Even quicker and easier, use a garlic press.

SUGAR SNAP PEA STIR-FRY

SERVES 6
TAKES: 20 MIN.

- 1 lb. fresh sugar snap peas
- 2 tsp. canola oil
- 1 garlic clove, minced
- 2 tsp. minced fresh gingerroot
- 1½ tsp. balsamic vinegar
- 1½ tsp. reduced-sodium soy sauce
- 1 tsp. sesame oil
- Dash cayenne pepper
- 1 Tbsp. minced fresh basil or 1 tsp. dried basil
- 2 tsp. sesame seeds, toasted

In the Titan Pan, saute the peas in canola oil until crisp-tender. Add the garlic, ginger, vinegar, soy sauce, sesame oil and cayenne; saute 1 minute longer. Add basil; toss to combine. Sprinkle with sesame seeds.

½ CUP *60 cal., 3g fat (0 sat. fat), 0 chol., 59mg sod., 6g carb. (3g sugars, 2g fiber), 3g pro.*

BOK CHOY & RADISH BOWLS

SERVES 8
TAKES: 25 MIN.

- 1 head bok choy
- 2 Tbsp. butter
- 1 Tbsp. olive oil
- 12 radishes, thinly sliced
- 1 shallot, sliced
- 1 tsp. lemon-pepper seasoning
- ¾ tsp. salt

Cut off and discard root end of bok choy, leaving stalks with leaves. Cut green leaves from stalks and cut the leaves into 1-in. slices; set aside. Cut the white stalks into 1-in. pieces.

In the Titan Pan, cook bok choy stalks in butter and oil until crisp-tender, 3-5 minutes. Add the radishes, shallot, lemon pepper, salt and sliced leaves; cook and stir until heated through, 3 minutes. Serve in individual bowls.

¾ CUP *59 cal., 5g fat (2g sat. fat), 8mg chol., 371mg sod., 3g carb. (2g sugars, 1g fiber), 2g pro.*

HERBED NOODLES WITH EDAMAME

HERBED NOODLES WITH EDAMAME

SERVES 4

TAKES: 30 MIN.

- 3½ cups uncooked egg noodles
- 2 Tbsp. butter
- 1 green onion, sliced
- 1 Tbsp. finely chopped sweet red pepper
- ½ cup frozen shelled edamame, thawed
- ¼ cup reduced-sodium chicken broth
- 1 Tbsp. minced fresh parsley
- 1½ tsp. minced fresh marjoram
- 1½ tsp. minced fresh chives
- 1 Tbsp. olive oil
- ¼ cup grated Romano cheese

Cook noodles in the Titan Pan according to package directions. Drain and set aside.

In the pan, heat butter over medium-high heat. Add onion and red pepper; cook and stir until tender. Stir in edamame and broth; heat through. Add herbs. Add noodles; toss to combine. Cook and stir until heated through, 1-2 minutes. Transfer to a serving plate. Drizzle with oil and sprinkle with cheese.

1 CUP *264 cal., 14g fat (6g sat. fat), 50mg chol., 214mg sod., 26g carb. (1g sugars, 2g fiber), 10g pro.*

PROSCIUTTO & PEA MEDLEY

SERVES 4
TAKES: 20 MIN.

- 1 Tbsp. olive oil
- 4 to 8 thin slices prosciutto, julienned
- ½ cup sliced fresh shiitake mushrooms
- 2 cups frozen peas, thawed
- 1 small onion, chopped

In the Titan Pan, heat oil over medium heat. Add prosciutto; cook until crisp, stirring occasionally. Remove with a slotted spoon; drain on paper towels. Cook and stir mushrooms, peas and onion in drippings until tender, 5-7 minutes. Sprinkle with prosciutto.

¾ CUP *122 cal., 5g fat (1g sat. fat), 13mg chol., 349mg sod., 11g carb. (4g sugars, 4g fiber), 8g pro.*

COZY GINGER CRUMB CAKE

SERVES 16

PREP: 20 MIN. BAKE: 35 MIN.

- 4 cups all-purpose flour
- 2 cups sugar
- 1 cup cold butter
- ½ tsp. ground ginger
- ¼ tsp. ground cloves
- ½ tsp. ground cinnamon
- ½ tsp. ground nutmeg
- 1 cup plus 2 Tbsp. buttermilk
- 1¼ tsp. baking soda
- 2 large eggs, room temperature
- Confectioners' sugar, optional

Preheat oven to 350°. In a large bowl, combine flour and sugar; cut in the butter until crumbly. Set aside 2 cups. Combine the remaining crumb mixture with the remaining ingredients.

Sprinkle 1 cup reserved crumbs into a greased Titan Pan. Pour batter over the crumbs; sprinkle with the remaining crumbs. Bake until a toothpick inserted in the center comes out clean, about 35 minutes. If desired, sprinkle with confectioners' sugar.

1 PIECE *330 cal., 13g fat (8g sat. fat), 54mg chol., 232mg sod., 50g carb. (26g sugars, 1g fiber), 5g pro.*

CARAMEL RHUBARB COBBLER

SERVES 6

PREP: 25 MIN. BAKE: 35 MIN.

- 7 Tbsp. butter, divided
- ¾ cup packed brown sugar
- ½ cup sugar, divided
- 3 Tbsp. cornstarch
- 1¼ cups water
- 6 cups chopped fresh or frozen rhubarb, thawed
- 3 to 4 drops red food coloring, optional
- 1¼ cups all-purpose flour
- 1½ tsp. baking powder
- ¼ tsp. salt
- ⅓ cup 2% milk
- Cinnamon-sugar
- Whipped cream or ice cream, optional

In the Titan Pan over medium heat, melt 3 Tbsp. butter. Add the brown sugar, ¼ cup sugar and the cornstarch. Gradually stir in water and rhubarb; cook and stir until thickened, 5-8 minutes. Add food coloring if desired. Remove from heat and set aside.

In another bowl, combine flour, baking powder, salt and the remaining ¼ cup sugar. Melt the remaining 4 Tbsp. butter; add to dry ingredients with milk. Mix well. Drop by tablespoonfuls onto the rhubarb mixture. Bake at 350° for 35-40 minutes or until the fruit is bubbly and the top is golden brown. Sprinkle with cinnamon-sugar. Serve warm, with whipped cream or ice cream if desired.

1 SERVING *429 cal., 14g fat (9g sat. fat), 38mg chol., 357mg sod., 73g carb. (47g sugars, 3g fiber), 4g pro.*

BERRY BROWNIE PIZZA

SERVES 12

PREP: 15 MIN. BAKE: 15 MIN. + CHILLING

- 1 pkg. fudge brownie mix (8-in. square pan size)
- 1¼ cups cold 2% milk
- 1 pkg. (3.4 oz.) instant vanilla pudding mix
- 2½ cups whipped topping
- 2 cups mixed fresh berries
- Chocolate syrup and chopped pecans

Prepare brownie batter according to the package directions. Lightly grease the bottom of the Titan Pan; add batter and spread evenly.

Bake at 350° until a toothpick inserted in the center comes out almost clean, 18-22 minutes. Cool for 15 minutes on a wire rack.

Meanwhile, in a large bowl, whisk milk and pudding mix for 2 minutes. Let stand until soft-set, about 2 minutes. Fold in whipped topping. Spread over brownie crust.

Top with berries and drizzle with chocolate syrup. Sprinkle with pecans. Refrigerate until chilled.

1 PIECE *312 cal., 14g fat (5g sat. fat), 19mg chol., 215mg sod., 44g carb. (31g sugars, 2g fiber), 4g pro.*

CHEF TIP

Don't wash blueberries more than 1 day before using or they may mold.

GIANT CHOCOLATE PECAN COOKIE

SERVES 12
PREP: 15 MIN. BAKE: 35 MIN.

- 1 cup butter
- 1 cup sugar
- 1 cup packed brown sugar
- 2 large eggs, room temperature
- 2 tsp. vanilla extract
- 3 cups all-purpose flour
- 1½ tsp. baking soda
- ½ tsp. kosher salt
- 1 cup 60% cacao bittersweet chocolate baking chips
- 1 cup chopped pecans, toasted
- Vanilla ice cream, optional

Preheat oven to 350°. In the Titan Pan, heat butter in oven as it preheats. Meanwhile, in a large bowl, stir together sugar and brown sugar. When butter is almost melted, remove pan from oven and swirl butter until completely melted. Stir butter into sugar mixture; set pan aside.

Beat eggs and vanilla into sugar mixture. In another bowl, whisk together flour, baking soda and salt; gradually beat into sugar mixture. Stir in chocolate chips and nuts. Spread mixture into buttered pan.

Bake until toothpick inserted in center comes out with moist crumbs and top is golden brown, 35-40 minutes. Serve warm, with vanilla ice cream if desired.

1 SERVING *528 cal., 27g fat (13g sat. fat), 72mg chol., 378mg sod., 69g carb. (43g sugars, 3g fiber), 6g pro.*

STRAWBERRY BUTTERMILK SHORTCAKE

SERVES 10

PREP: 25 MIN. BAKE: 50 MIN.

- 10 Tbsp. shortening
- ¼ cup butter, softened
- 1 cup sugar
- 2 large eggs, room temperature
- 2½ cups all-purpose flour
- 3 tsp. baking powder
- ½ tsp. salt
- ⅔ cup buttermilk

STREUSEL TOPPING

- ⅔ cup all-purpose flour
- ½ cup sugar
- 1 tsp. ground cinnamon
- ¼ tsp. ground allspice
- ½ cup butter, softened
- 2 cups sliced fresh strawberries
- Whipped cream

Preheat oven to 350°. In a large bowl, cream the shortening, butter and sugar until light and fluffy, 5-7 minutes. Add eggs, 1 at a time, beating well after each addition. In another bowl, whisk flour, baking powder and salt; add to creamed mixture alternately with buttermilk, beating well after each addition. Transfer to the Titan Pan.

For streusel topping, in a small bowl, mix flour, sugar, cinnamon and allspice; cut in butter until crumbly. Sprinkle over batter. Top with strawberries. Bake until center is puffed and edges are golden brown, 50-60 minutes. Serve warm with whipped cream.

1 SLICE *526 cal., 27g fat (12g sat. fat), 74mg chol., 418mg sod., 64g carb. (33g sugars, 2g fiber), 6g pro.*

CHEF TIP

Look for brightly colored, plump and fragrant strawberries with the green hulls intact. Avoid any that are soft, shriveled or moldy. Wash berries before removing hulls. One pint of strawberries yields 1½-2 cups sliced.

CHAPTER 2

SUMMER

BREAKFAST

SMALL PLATES

MAIN COURSES

SIDES

DESSERTS

BLUEBERRY-STUFFED FRENCH TOAST

SERVES 8

PREP: 35 MIN. BAKE: 15 MIN./BATCH

- 1½ cups fresh or frozen blueberries
- 3 Tbsp. sugar, divided
- 8 slices Italian bread (1¼ in. thick)
- 4 large eggs
- 1 tsp. grated orange zest
- ½ cup orange juice
- Dash salt

SAUCE

- ¼ cup orange juice
- ¼ cup water
- 3 Tbsp. sugar
- 1 Tbsp. cornstarch
- ⅛ tsp. salt
- 1½ cups orange sections
- 1 cup fresh or frozen blueberries
- ⅓ cup sliced almonds, toasted

Preheat oven to 400°. In a small bowl, toss blueberries with 2 Tbsp. sugar. Cut a pocket horizontally in each slice of bread; fill with blueberries.

In a shallow bowl, whisk eggs, orange zest, orange juice, salt and remaining sugar. Working in batches of 4, dip both sides of each bread slice into egg mixture, being careful to not squeeze out berries. Place in a lightly greased Titan Pan. Bake until golden brown, 14-17 minutes, carefully turning once. Remove and keep warm. Repeat with remaining stuffed bread slices and egg mixture.

In the same pan, whisk the first 5 sauce ingredients until smooth. Bring to a boil, stirring constantly; cook and stir 1-2 minutes or until thickened. Reduce heat; stir in fruit and heat through. Serve with French toast; sprinkle with almonds.

1 SLICE WITH ¼ CUP SAUCE AND 2 TSP. ALMONDS
167 cal., 5g fat (1g sat. fat), 106mg chol., 118mg sod., 27g carb. (19g sugars, 3g fiber), 5g pro.

GARDEN CHEDDAR FRITTATA

SERVES 6

PREP: 30 MIN. BAKE: 15 MIN.

- 2 small potatoes, peeled and cut into ½-in. cubes
- 8 large eggs, lightly beaten
- 2 Tbsp. water
- ¼ tsp. salt
- ⅛ tsp. garlic powder
- ⅛ tsp. chili powder
- ⅛ tsp. pepper
- 1 small zucchini, chopped
- ¼ cup chopped onion
- 1 Tbsp. butter
- 1 Tbsp. olive oil
- 2 plum tomatoes, thinly sliced
- 1 cup shredded sharp cheddar cheese
- Minced chives and additional shredded cheddar cheese

Preheat oven to 425°. Place potatoes in the Titan Pan and cover with water. Bring to a boil. Reduce heat; cover and simmer 5 minutes. Drain. In a large bowl, whisk eggs, water, salt, garlic powder, chili powder and pepper; set aside.

In the pan, saute zucchini, onion and potatoes in butter and oil until tender. Reduce heat. Pour 1½ cups egg mixture into pan. Arrange half of the tomato slices over top; sprinkle with ½ cup cheese. Top with remaining egg mixture, tomato slices and cheese.

Bake, uncovered, until the eggs are completely set, 12-15 minutes. Let stand 5 minutes. Sprinkle with chives and additional cheddar cheese. Cut into wedges.

1 SLICE *251 cal., 16g fat (8g sat. fat), 307mg chol., 325mg sod., 13g carb. (3g sugars, 2g fiber), 14g pro.*

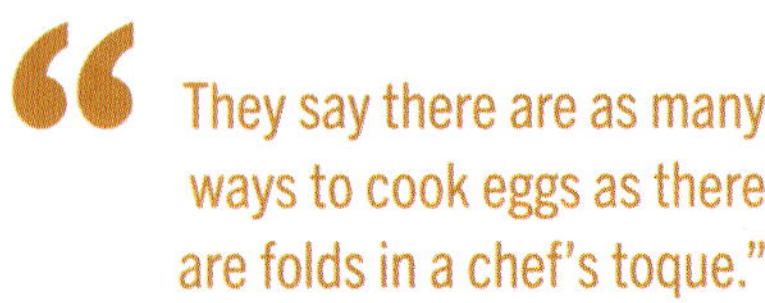

CORN CAKES WITH EGGS & MANGO SALSA

SERVES 6

PREP: 40 MIN. COOK: 5 MIN./BATCH

- 1 medium mango, peeled and chopped
- ½ cup salsa
- 2 Tbsp. minced fresh cilantro
- 1 green onion, finely chopped

CORN CAKES

- 4 large eggs, room temperature, divided use
- ⅔ cup all-purpose flour
- ⅔ cup cornmeal
- 4 tsp. baking powder
- 1 tsp. salt
- ⅛ tsp. pepper
- 1 can (8¼ oz.) cream-style corn
- ½ cup 2% milk
- ½ cup butter, melted
- 1 cup fresh or frozen corn, thawed
- 4 green onions, chopped
- ¼ tsp. cream of tartar

POACHED EGGS

- 1 Tbsp. white vinegar
- 6 large eggs

In a small bowl, combine the mango, salsa, cilantro and onion; set aside.

Separate 2 eggs. In a large bowl, combine the flour, cornmeal, baking powder, salt and pepper. In another bowl, whisk the remaining eggs, egg yolks, cream-style corn, milk and butter. Stir into dry ingredients just until blended. Fold in fresh corn and onions. In a small bowl, beat egg whites and cream of tartar until stiff peaks form. Fold into batter.

Pour batter by ¼ cupfuls into a greased Titan Pan. Cook on each side until golden brown, 2-3 minutes. Remove and keep warm. Wipe pan clean.

Pour 2-3 in. water into the Titan Pan; add vinegar. Bring to a boil; reduce heat and simmer gently. Break cold eggs, 1 at a time, into a custard cup or saucer; holding the cup close to the surface of the water, slip each egg into water.

Cook, uncovered, until whites are completely set and yolks are still soft, about 4 minutes. With a slotted spoon, lift eggs out of water. Serve with corn cakes and salsa.

1 SERVING *455 cal., 25g fat (13g sat. fat), 392mg chol., 1097mg sod., 45g carb. (10g sugars, 4g fiber), 16g pro.*

NUTTY DOUGHNUT NUGGETS

SERVES 16

PREP: 30 MIN. COOK: 5 MIN./BATCH

- 1 large egg
- 1 Tbsp. water
- 1 tube (16.3 oz.) large refrigerated flaky biscuits (8 count)
- ⅔ cup Nutella®
- Oil for deep-fat frying
- Confectioners' sugar

Whisk egg with water. On a lightly floured surface, roll each biscuit into a 6-in. circle; cut each circle into 4 wedges. Brush lightly with egg mixture; top each wedge with 1 tsp. Nutella®. Bring up corners over filling; pinch edges firmly to seal.

In the Titan Pan, heat 1 in. oil to 350°. In small batches, place doughnuts in hot oil, seam side down; fry until golden brown, 1-2 minutes per side. Drain on paper towels. Dust with confectioners' sugar; serve warm.

2 DOUGHNUTS *198 cal., 13g fat (2g sat. fat), 12mg chol., 283mg sod., 20g carb. (9g sugars, 1g fiber), 3g pro.*

FRESH CORN OMELET

SERVES 4
TAKES: 25 MIN.

- 10 large eggs
- 2 Tbsp. water
- ¼ tsp. salt
- ¼ tsp. pepper
- 2 tsp. plus 2 Tbsp. butter, divided
- 1 cup fresh or frozen corn, thawed
- ½ cup shredded cheddar cheese
- Fresh salsa

In a small bowl, whisk eggs, water, salt and pepper until blended. In the Titan Pan, heat 2 tsp. butter over medium heat. Add corn; cook and stir 1-2 minutes or until tender. Remove from pan.

In same pan, heat 1 Tbsp. butter over medium-high heat. Pour in half of the egg mixture. Mixture should set immediately at edges. As eggs set, push cooked portions toward the center, letting uncooked eggs flow underneath. When eggs are thickened and no liquid egg remains, spoon half of the corn onto 1 side; sprinkle with ¼ cup cheese. Fold omelet in half. Cut in half; slide each half onto a plate. Keep warm.

Repeat with remaining butter, egg mixture, corn and cheese. Serve with salsa.

½ OMELET *336 cal., 25g fat (12g sat. fat), 500mg chol., 482mg sod., 8g carb. (3g sugars, 1g fiber), 20g pro.*

FLAVORFUL BEEF FLAUTAS

SERVES 20

PREP: 1 HOUR 20 MIN. COOK: 5 MIN./BATCH

- 2½ tsp. canola oil
- 2 lbs. fresh beef brisket
- 2 medium onions, chopped
- 2 medium green peppers, chopped
- 2 cups water
- 1 tsp. salt
- 1 tsp. dried oregano
- 1 tsp. dried marjoram
- 1 tsp. pepper
- 20 corn tortillas (6 in.)
- Oil for deep-fat frying
- Optional toppings: Guacamole, sour cream and salsa

In the Titan Pan, heat 2½ tsp. oil over medium heat. Brown brisket on all sides. Add onions, peppers, water and seasonings. Bring to a boil. Reduce heat; simmer, covered, 1-1½ hours or until meat is tender.

Remove meat; cool slightly. Shred meat with 2 forks. Drain onion mixture; add to meat. Wrap tortillas in paper towel and microwave on high 20-30 seconds or just until warmed. Spoon ¼ cup beef mixture down the center of each tortilla. Roll up and secure with toothpicks. Wipe pan clean.

In the Titan Pan, heat 1 in. oil to 375°. Fry flautas, in batches, for 1 minute on each side or until golden brown. Drain on paper towels. Remove toothpicks. If desired, serve with toppings.

1 FLAUTA *162 cal., 8g fat (1g sat. fat), 19mg chol., 145mg sod., 12g carb. (1g sugars, 2g fiber), 11g pro.*

“Taste your food often as you’re cooking. The more you taste, the more you teach your palate how flavors change throughout the cooking process.”

ORANGE SHRIMP MOJO

SERVES 8

PREP: 25 MIN. COOK: 45 MIN.

- 1 Tbsp. cumin seeds
- 1 Tbsp. whole peppercorns
- 1 Tbsp. grated orange or tangerine zest
- ½ tsp. dried oregano
- ½ tsp. salt
- 1 lb. uncooked jumbo shrimp, peeled and deveined
- 4 tsp. olive oil
- 3 cups orange juice
- 3 Tbsp. rum or chicken broth
- 1 garlic clove, minced
- 1 large navel orange, peeled, sectioned and chopped
- ½ cup chopped sweet onion
- 1 cup cubed avocado
- ½ cup minced fresh cilantro, divided
- 1 tsp. chopped seeded jalapeno pepper

In the Titan Pan over medium heat, toast cumin seeds and peppercorns until aromatic, 1-2 minutes. Remove from pan. Crush seeds using a spice grinder or mortar and pestle.

In a small bowl, combine the orange zest, oregano, salt and crushed spices. Sprinkle 1 Tbsp. spice mixture over shrimp.

In the Titan Pan, cook shrimp in oil over medium-high heat for 1 minute; turn shrimp. Add orange juice, rum, garlic and 1 Tbsp. spice mixture. Cook and stir until shrimp turn pink, 1-2 minutes longer; remove shrimp and keep warm.

Bring liquid in pan to a boil. Cook until reduced to ⅔ cup, about 35 minutes. Meanwhile, for the salsa, combine orange, onion, avocado, ¼ cup cilantro, jalapeno and remaining spice mixture in a small bowl.

Stir shrimp and remaining cilantro into sauce; heat through. Serve with salsa.

1 SERVING *172 cal., 6g fat (1g sat. fat), 69mg chol., 218mg sod., 16g carb. (11g sugars, 2g fiber), 11g pro.*

CHILI-LIME CHICKEN WINGS

SERVES 12

PREP: 20 MIN. COOK: 10 MIN./BATCH

- 2½ lbs. whole chicken wings
- 1 cup maple syrup
- ⅔ cup chili sauce
- 2 Tbsp. lime juice
- 2 Tbsp. Dijon mustard
- 1 cup all-purpose flour
- 2 tsp. salt
- 2 tsp. paprika
- ¼ tsp. pepper
- Oil for deep-fat frying
- Thinly sliced green onions and lime wedges, optional

Cut wings into 3 sections; discard wing tip sections. In the Titan Pan, combine the syrup, chili sauce, lime juice and mustard. Bring to a boil; cook until liquid is reduced to about 1 cup. Pour sauce into a large bowl and set aside. Wipe pan clean.

Meanwhile, in a large shallow dish, combine the flour, salt, paprika and pepper. Add wings a few at a time and toss to coat.

In the Titan Pan, heat 1 in. oil to 375°. Fry wings, a few at a time, for 6-8 minutes or until no longer pink, turning once. Drain on paper towels. Transfer wings to sauce mixture and toss to coat. Serve immediately, with sliced green onions and lime wedges if desired.

2 PIECES *285 cal., 17g fat (3g sat. fat), 31mg chol., 395mg sod., 24g carb. (19g sugars, 0 fiber), 10g pro.*

WINGETTE IT!

TWO EASY STEPS

Place chicken wing on a cutting board. With a sharp knife, cut between the joint at the top of the tip end. (Discard the tip or use for making broth.) • Take the remaining wing and cut between the joints. Proceed with the recipe as directed.

FRIED GREEN TOMATO NAPOLEONS WITH SLAW

SERVES 4

PREP: 30 MIN. COOK: 5 MIN.

- ⅓ cup mayonnaise
- ¼ cup white vinegar
- 2 Tbsp. sugar
- 1 tsp. salt
- 1 tsp. garlic powder
- ½ tsp. pepper
- 1 pkg. (14 oz.) three-color coleslaw mix
- ¼ cup finely chopped onion
- 1 can (11 oz.) mandarin oranges, drained

FRIED TOMATOES

- 1 large egg, lightly beaten
- Dash hot pepper sauce, or to taste
- ¼ cup all-purpose flour
- 1 cup dry bread crumbs
- 2 medium green tomatoes, cut into 4 slices each
- Oil for frying
- ½ tsp. salt
- ¼ tsp. pepper

TOPPINGS

- ½ cup pimiento cheese spread
- 4 tsp. pepper jelly

Combine the first 6 ingredients. Add coleslaw mix and onion. Add mandarin oranges; stir carefully.

In a shallow bowl, whisk egg and hot sauce. Place the flour and bread crumbs in separate shallow bowls. Dip tomato slices into flour to coat both sides; shake off excess. Dip into egg mixture, then into bread crumbs, patting to help coating adhere.

In the Titan Pan, heat ¼ in. oil to 350°. Fry tomato slices, a few at a time, until browned, 1-2 minutes on each side. Drain on paper towels. Sprinkle with salt and pepper.

To assemble napoleons, layer 1 tomato slice with 1 Tbsp. pimiento cheese. Repeat layers. Top with 1 tsp. pepper jelly. Repeat with remaining tomato slices. Serve over coleslaw.

1 SERVING *487 cal., 31g fat (7g sat. fat), 22mg chol., 1281mg sod., 45g carb. (26g sugars, 5g fiber), 7g pro.*

BANG BANG SHRIMP CAKE SLIDERS

SERVES 12
PREP: 30 MIN. + CHILLING COOK: 10 MIN./BATCH

- 1 lb. uncooked shrimp (41-50 per lb.), peeled and deveined
- 1 large egg, lightly beaten
- ½ cup finely chopped sweet red pepper
- 6 green onions, chopped and divided
- 1 Tbsp. minced fresh gingerroot
- ¼ tsp. salt
- 1 cup panko bread crumbs
- ¼ cup mayonnaise
- 1 Tbsp. Sriracha chili sauce
- 1 Tbsp. sweet chili sauce
- 5 cups shredded Chinese or napa cabbage
- 3 Tbsp. canola oil
- 12 mini buns or dinner rolls, toasted
- Additional Sriracha chili sauce, optional

Place shrimp in a food processor; pulse until chopped. In a large bowl, combine the egg, red pepper, 4 green onions, ginger and salt. Add shrimp and bread crumbs; mix gently. Shape into twelve ½-in.-thick patties. Refrigerate at least 20 minutes.

Meanwhile, in a large bowl, combine mayonnaise and the chili sauces; stir in cabbage and the remaining green onions.

In the Titan Pan, heat oil over medium heat. Add shrimp cakes in batches; cook until golden brown on each side, 4-5 minutes. Serve on toasted buns with slaw; secure with toothpicks. If desired, serve with additional chili sauce.

1 SLIDER *210 cal., 10g fat (1g sat. fat), 63mg chol., 321mg sod., 20g carb. (3g sugars, 1g fiber), 11g pro.*

SPICY CHICKEN FAJITAS

SERVES 6

PREP: 20 MIN. + MARINATING COOK: 10 MIN.

- 4 Tbsp. canola oil, divided
- 2 Tbsp. lemon juice
- 1½ tsp. seasoned salt
- 1½ tsp. dried oregano
- 1½ tsp. ground cumin
- 1 tsp. garlic powder
- ½ tsp. chili powder
- ½ tsp. paprika
- ½ tsp. crushed red pepper flakes, optional
- 1½ lbs. boneless skinless chicken breast, cut into thin strips
- ½ medium sweet red pepper, julienned
- ½ medium green pepper, julienned
- 4 green onions, thinly sliced
- ½ cup chopped onion
- 6 flour tortillas (8 in.), warmed
- Optional toppings: Shredded cheddar cheese, taco sauce, salsa, guacamole and sour cream

In a large bowl, combine 2 Tbsp. oil, lemon juice and seasonings; add the chicken. Turn to coat; cover. Refrigerate 1-4 hours.

In the Titan Pan, saute peppers and onions in the remaining 2 Tbsp. oil until crisp-tender. Remove and keep warm.

Drain chicken, discarding marinade. In the same pan, cook chicken over medium-high heat until no longer pink, 5-6 minutes. Return pepper mixture to the pan; heat through.

Spoon filling down the center of tortillas; fold in half. If desired, serve with toppings.

1 FAJITA *369 cal., 15g fat (2g sat. fat), 63mg chol., 689mg sod., 30g carb. (2g sugars, 1g fiber), 28g pro.*

PEPPER STEAK WITH SQUASH

SERVES 6
TAKES: 30 MIN.

- 1 can (14½ oz.) reduced-sodium beef broth
- 2 Tbsp. reduced-sodium soy sauce
- 3 Tbsp. cornstarch
- 2 Tbsp. canola oil, divided
- 1 beef flank steak (1 lb.), cut into thin strips
- 1 medium green pepper, cut into thin strips
- 1 medium sweet red pepper, cut into thin strips
- 2 medium zucchini, cut into thin strips
- 1 small onion, cut into thin strips
- 3 garlic cloves, minced
- 1 cup fresh snow peas
- 1 cup sliced fresh mushrooms
- 1 can (8 oz.) sliced water chestnuts, drained
- Hot cooked rice

Mix broth and soy sauce with cornstarch until smooth. Set aside.

In the Titan Pan, heat 1 Tbsp. oil over medium-high heat. Add the beef; stir-fry until no longer pink, 2-3 minutes. Remove from pan.

In same pan, heat remaining oil. Stir-fry peppers about 2 minutes. Add zucchini, onion and garlic; cook and stir 2 minutes longer. Add snow peas, mushrooms and water chestnuts. Stir-fry until crisp-tender, about 2 minutes more.

Stir cornstarch mixture and add to pan. Bring to a boil; cook and stir until sauce is thickened, 1-2 minutes. Return beef to skillet; heat through. Serve with hot cooked rice.

1½ CUPS STIR-FRY *229 cal., 11g fat (3g sat. fat), 37mg chol., 381mg sod., 16g carb. (5g sugars, 3g fiber), 18g pro.*

APPLESAUCE BARBECUE CHICKEN

SERVES 4
TAKES: 20 MIN.

- 4 boneless skinless chicken breast halves (6 oz. each)
- ½ tsp. pepper
- 1 Tbsp. olive oil
- ⅔ cup chunky applesauce
- ⅔ cup spicy barbecue sauce
- 2 Tbsp. brown sugar
- 1 tsp. chili powder

Sprinkle chicken with pepper. In the Titan Pan, brown chicken in oil on both sides. In a small bowl, combine the remaining ingredients; pour over chicken. Cover and cook until a thermometer reads 165°, 7-10 minutes.

Freeze option Cool chicken; transfer to a freezer container and freeze for up to 3 months. Thaw in the refrigerator overnight. Place in the Titan Pan; cover and cook on medium-high heat until heated through, 8-10 minutes, stirring once.

1 CHICKEN BREAST HALF *308 cal., 8g fat (2g sat. fat), 94mg chol., 473mg sod., 22g carb. (19g sugars, 1g fiber), 35g pro.*

"People say all sorts of things taste like chicken. Rabbit tastes like chicken and snake tastes like chicken. If that's the case, they're cooking chicken all wrong!"

PORK CHOPS WITH NECTARINE SAUCE

SERVES 4
TAKES: 30 MIN.

- 4 boneless pork loin chops (6 oz. each)
- ½ tsp. salt
- ½ tsp. dried thyme
- ¼ tsp. pepper
- 3 Tbsp. all-purpose flour
- 1 Tbsp. canola oil
- 1 small onion, finely chopped
- 1 garlic clove, minced
- 3 medium nectarines or peeled peaches, cut into ½-in. slices
- ½ cup reduced-sodium chicken broth
- 1 Tbsp. honey, optional

Sprinkle pork chops with seasonings. Dredge lightly with flour. In the Titan Pan, heat oil over medium heat; cook pork chops until a thermometer reads 145°, 4-5 minutes per side. Remove from pan; keep warm.

Add onion to pan; cook and stir over medium heat 2 minutes. Add garlic; cook and stir 1 minute. Add nectarines; cook until lightly browned on both sides. Stir in broth and, if desired, honey; bring to a boil. Reduce heat; simmer, uncovered, until nectarines are softened and sauce is slightly thickened, about 5 minutes. Serve with chops.

1 PORK CHOP WITH ½ CUP SAUCE *330 cal., 14g fat (4g sat. fat), 82mg chol., 414mg sod., 16g carb. (9g sugars, 2g fiber), 35g pro.*

SALMON WITH MANGO-CITRUS SALSA

SERVES 4
TAKES: 30 MIN.

- 1 large navel orange
- 1 medium lemon
- 2 Tbsp. olive oil
- 1 Tbsp. capers, drained and coarsely chopped
- 1½ tsp. minced fresh mint
- 1½ tsp. minced fresh parsley
- ¼ tsp. crushed red pepper flakes
- ⅛ tsp. plus ½ tsp. salt, divided
- ⅛ tsp. plus ¼ tsp. pepper, divided
- 1 medium mango, peeled and chopped
- 1 green onion, thinly sliced
- 4 salmon fillets (6 oz. each)
- 1 Tbsp. canola oil

For salsa, finely grate enough zest from the orange to measure 2 tsp.; finely grate enough zest from the lemon to measure ½ tsp. Place citrus zests in a small bowl. Cut lemon crosswise in half; squeeze 2 Tbsp. lemon juice and add to bowl.

Cut a thin slice from the top and bottom of the orange; stand orange upright on a cutting board. With a knife, cut off peel and outer membrane from orange. Cut along the membrane of each segment to remove fruit.

Add olive oil, capers, mint, parsley, pepper flakes and ⅛ tsp. each salt and pepper to lemon juice mixture. Gently stir in mango, green onion and orange sections.

Sprinkle salmon with the remaining salt and pepper. In the Titan Pan, heat canola oil over medium heat. Add salmon; cook 5-6 minutes on each side or until fish just begins to flake easily with a fork. Serve with salsa.

1 FILLET WITH ½ CUP SALSA *433 cal., 26g fat (4g sat. fat), 85mg chol., 516mg sod., 19g carb. (16g sugars, 3g fiber), 30g pro.*

> "The keys to working with seafood are practice and repetition. From cutting to cooking, you have to do it a lot of times to build that muscle memory."

THREE-BEAN BAKED BEANS

SERVES 12
PREP: 20 MIN. BAKE: 1 HOUR

- ½ lb. ground beef
- 5 bacon strips, diced
- ½ cup chopped onion
- ⅓ cup packed brown sugar
- ¼ cup sugar
- ¼ cup ketchup
- ¼ cup barbecue sauce
- 2 Tbsp. molasses
- 2 Tbsp. prepared mustard
- ½ tsp. chili powder
- ½ tsp. salt
- 2 cans (16 oz. each) pork and beans, undrained
- 1 can (16 oz.) butter beans, rinsed and drained
- 1 can (16 oz.) kidney beans, rinsed and drained

Preheat oven to 350°. In the Titan Pan, cook and crumble beef with bacon and onion over medium heat until beef is no longer pink; drain.

Stir in sugars, ketchup, barbecue sauce, molasses, mustard, chili powder and salt until blended. Stir in the beans. Bake, covered, until beans reach desired thickness, about 1 hour.

Freeze option Freeze cooled bean mixture in freezer containers. To use, partially thaw in the refrigerator overnight. Heat through in the Titan Pan, stirring occasionally and adding a little water if necessary.

¾ CUP *269 cal., 8g fat (2g sat. fat), 19mg chol., 708mg sod., 42g carb. (21g sugars, 7g fiber), 13g pro.*

THREE-BEAN BAKED BEANS

BALSAMIC-GLAZED ZUCCHINI

BALSAMIC-GLAZED ZUCCHINI

SERVES 4
TAKES: 15 MIN.

- 1 Tbsp. olive oil
- 3 medium zucchini, cut into ½-in. slices
- 2 garlic cloves, minced
- ¼ tsp. salt
- ¼ cup balsamic vinegar

In the Titan Pan, heat oil over medium-high heat. Add zucchini; cook and stir until tender, 5-7 minutes. Add garlic and salt; cook 1 minute longer. Remove from the pan.

Add vinegar to pan; bring to a boil. Cook until reduced by half. Add zucchini; toss to coat.

⅔ CUP *65 cal., 4g fat (1g sat. fat), 0 chol., 166mg sod., 8g carb. (5g sugars, 2g fiber), 2g pro.*

SOUTHERN GREEN BEANS WITH APRICOTS

SERVES 8

PREP: 15 MIN. COOK: 10 MIN.

- 2 lbs. fresh green beans, trimmed
- 1 can (14½ oz.) chicken broth
- ½ lb. bacon strips, chopped
- 1 cup dried apricots, chopped
- ¼ cup balsamic vinegar
- ¾ tsp. salt
- ¾ tsp. garlic powder
- ¾ tsp. pepper

Place green beans and broth in the Titan Pan. Bring to a boil. Cook, covered, until beans are crisp-tender, 4-7 minutes; drain and set beans aside.

In pan, cook chopped bacon over medium heat until crisp, stirring occasionally. Remove with a slotted spoon; drain on paper towels. Pour off all but 1 Tbsp. drippings.

Add apricots to pan; cook and stir over medium heat until softened. Stir in vinegar, salt, garlic powder, pepper and beans; cook and stir until beans are coated, 2-3 minutes longer. Sprinkle with bacon.

¾ CUP *149 cal., 6g fat (2g sat. fat), 12mg chol., 464mg sod., 21g carb. (14g sugars, 5g fiber), 6g pro.*

BALSAMIC VINEGAR FYI

Over the years, balsamic vinegar has gone from an exotic ingredient to a pantry staple. Dark, thick and sweet-smelling, this Italian vinegar adds a rich color to dishes during cooking. There's also white balsamic vinegar if you prefer a lighter color.

No matter the hue, balsamic vinegars come in a range of prices. As with wine, the grapes, processing, aging method and aging time all contribute to the cost. Higher-priced balsamics are best drizzled over cooked foods as a finishing touch.

SOUTHERN GREEN BEANS WITH APRICOTS

SAUTEED SQUASH STIR-UP

SAUTEED SQUASH STIR-UP

SERVES 8
TAKES: 20 MIN.

- 2 Tbsp. olive oil
- 1 medium onion, finely chopped
- 4 medium zucchini, chopped
- 2 large tomatoes, finely chopped
- 1 tsp. salt
- ¼ tsp. pepper

In the Titan Pan, heat oil over medium-high heat. Add onion; cook and stir until tender, 2-4 minutes. Add zucchini; cook and stir 3 minutes.

Stir in tomatoes, salt and pepper; cook and stir until squash is tender, 4-6 minutes longer. Serve with a slotted spoon.

¾ CUP *60 cal., 4g fat (1g sat. fat), 0 chol., 306mg sod., 6g carb. (4g sugars, 2g fiber), 2g pro.*

CARROT & KALE VEGETABLE SAUTE

SERVES 8

PREP: 15 MIN. COOK: 20 MIN.

- 8 bacon strips, coarsely chopped
- 4 large carrots, sliced
- 2 cups peeled cubed butternut squash (½-in. pieces)
- 1 poblano pepper, seeded and chopped
- ½ cup finely chopped red onion
- 1 tsp. smoked paprika
- ¼ tsp. salt
- ¼ tsp. pepper
- 2 plum tomatoes, chopped
- 2 cups chopped fresh kale

In the Titan Pan, cook chopped bacon over medium heat until crisp, stirring occasionally. Using a slotted spoon, remove bacon to paper towels. Pour off all but 1 Tbsp. drippings.

Add carrots and squash to drippings; cook, covered, over medium heat for 5 minutes. Add poblano pepper and onion; cook until vegetables are tender, about 5 minutes, stirring occasionally. Stir in seasonings. Add tomatoes and kale; cook, covered, until kale is wilted, 2-3 minutes. Top with bacon.

¾ CUP *101 cal., 5g fat (2g sat. fat), 10mg chol., 251mg sod., 11g carb. (4g sugars, 3g fiber), 4g pro.*

HOW TO

TRIM KALE

If kale is thin and tender, pull the leaves from the stems or remove them with kitchen shears. • If the stems are thicker, place on a cutting board, fold the leaf in half and use a knife to slice away the stem. Discard the stem. Carefully chop leaves as desired or as instructed in the recipe at hand.

FRESH FRUIT COBBLER

SERVES 12
PREP: 15 MIN. BAKE: 40 MIN.

- 5 to 6 cups chopped fresh fruit (apples, rhubarb, blueberries or peaches)
- 2 cups all-purpose flour
- ½ cup sugar
- 4 tsp. baking powder
- 1 tsp. salt
- ½ cup cold butter, cubed
- 1 cup 2% milk

TOPPING

- ⅔ cup sugar
- ¼ cup cornstarch
- 1½ cups boiling water

Arrange fruit evenly in the bottom of the Titan Pan.

In a bowl, combine flour, sugar, baking powder and salt; cut in butter until crumbly. Stir in milk. Spoon over the fruit. Combine sugar and cornstarch; sprinkle over the batter. Pour water over all. Bake at 350° for 40-45 minutes or until fruit is tender.

1 SERVING *272 cal., 8g fat (5g sat. fat), 22mg chol., 417mg sod., 47g carb. (27g sugars, 1g fiber), 3g pro.*

IS ORGANIC
NECESSARY?

The Environmental Working Group (*ewg.org*) lists the "Clean 15" fruits and vegetables that are lower in pesticides so you can skip the high prices of organic produce: onions, sweet corn, pineapples, avocados, asparagus, sweet peas (frozen), papayas, kiwi, eggplant, domestic cantaloupe, cabbage, cauliflower, honeydew, broccoli and mushrooms.

SOUR CREAM PEACH KUCHEN

SERVES 12

PREP: 15 MIN. BAKE: 45 MIN.

- 3 cups all-purpose flour
- 1¼ cups sugar, divided
- ½ tsp. baking powder
- ¼ tsp. salt
- 1 cup cold butter, cubed
- 2 cans (29 oz. each) sliced peaches, drained or 13 small peaches, peeled and sliced
- 1 tsp. ground cinnamon

TOPPING

- 4 large egg yolks
- 2 cups sour cream
- 2 to 3 Tbsp. sugar
- ¼ tsp. ground cinnamon

In a large bowl, combine the flour, ¼ cup sugar, baking powder and salt; cut in butter until mixture resembles coarse crumbs. Press onto the bottom and 1 in. up the sides of the Titan Pan.

Arrange peaches over crust. Combine cinnamon and remaining sugar; sprinkle over peaches. Bake at 400° for 15 minutes.

Meanwhile, in a small bowl, combine egg yolks and sour cream. Spread evenly over peaches. Combine sugar and cinnamon; sprinkle over top.

Bake 30-35 minutes longer or until set. Serve warm or cold. Store leftovers in the refrigerator.

1 PIECE *507 cal., 24g fat (15g sat. fat), 135mg chol., 197mg sod., 66g carb. (41g sugars, 2g fiber), 6g pro.*

GLAZED FRUIT PIZZA

SERVES 16

PREP: 25 MIN. + CHILLING BAKE: 10 MIN. + COOLING

- 1 cup all-purpose flour
- ¼ cup confectioners' sugar
- ½ cup cold butter, cubed

GLAZE

- 5 tsp. cornstarch
- 1¼ cups unsweetened pineapple juice
- 1 tsp. lemon juice

TOPPINGS

- 1 pkg. (8 oz.) reduced-fat cream cheese
- ⅓ cup sugar
- 1 tsp. vanilla extract
- 2 cups halved fresh strawberries
- 1 cup fresh blueberries
- 1 can (11 oz.) mandarin oranges, drained

Preheat oven to 350°. In a large bowl, mix flour and confectioners' sugar; cut in butter until crumbly. Press onto bottom of the Titan Pan. Bake until very lightly browned, 10-12 minutes. Cool completely on a wire rack. Remove from pan.

In pan, mix glaze ingredients until smooth; bring to a boil. Cook and stir until thickened, about 30 seconds. Cool slightly.

In a bowl, beat cream cheese, sugar and vanilla until smooth. Spread over crust. Top with berries and mandarin oranges. Drizzle with glaze. Refrigerate until cold.

1 SLICE *170 cal., 9g fat (6g sat. fat), 25mg chol., 120mg sod., 20g carb. (13g sugars, 1g fiber), 3g pro.*

HOW TO

HULL A STRAWBERRY

Insert a straw into the tip of the berry. • Push hull through the other end.

CHERRY-BLACKBERRY CRISP

SERVES 14

PREP: 20 MIN. + STANDING BAKE: 55 MIN.

- ⅔ cup packed brown sugar
- 2 Tbsp. quick-cooking tapioca
- ½ tsp. almond extract
- ¼ tsp. ground cinnamon
- 4 cups frozen pitted tart cherries, thawed
- 2 cups frozen unsweetened blackberries, thawed

TOPPING

- 1½ cups all-purpose flour
- 1½ cups sugar
- Dash salt
- ⅔ cup cold butter
- 1½ cups finely chopped walnuts
- Whipped cream

In a large bowl, combine the brown sugar, tapioca, extract and cinnamon. Gently stir in cherries and blackberries. Allow to stand for 10 minutes. Pour into the Titan Pan.

In another bowl, combine the flour, sugar and salt. Cut in butter until crumbly. Add walnuts; sprinkle over fruit. Bake, uncovered, at 350° for 55-60 minutes or until topping is golden brown and filling is bubbly. Serve warm with whipped cream.

1 SERVING *371 cal., 17g fat (6g sat. fat), 23mg chol., 77mg sod., 53g carb. (38g sugars, 3g fiber), 4g pro.*

TAKE YOUR PICK

Savor sweet and sour cherry varieties at peak season in summer. Here are some tips for picking the best of the bunch.

Check for Freshness Look for firm, plump, shiny cherries that are bright in color with green stems attached.

Favor a Flavor Sour cherries, such as Montmorency and Morello, are usually red and perfect for baking. Sweet varieties, such as Bing and Rainier, vary in color and make a delish on-the-go snack.

Keep Cold and Dry Cherries can last 7-10 days in the fridge, unwashed until ready for use.

CHAPTER 3

FALL

SAVORY APPLE-CHICKEN SAUSAGE

SAVORY APPLE-CHICKEN SAUSAGE

SERVES 8
TAKES: 25 MIN.

- 1 large tart apple, peeled and diced
- 2 tsp. poultry seasoning
- 1 tsp. salt
- ¼ tsp. pepper
- 1 lb. ground chicken

In a large bowl, combine the first 4 ingredients. Crumble chicken over the mixture and mix well. Shape into eight 3-in. patties.

In the Titan Pan, cook patties over medium heat until no longer pink, 5-6 minutes on each side. Drain if necessary.

1 SAUSAGE PATTY *92 cal., 5g fat (1g sat. fat), 38mg chol., 328mg sod., 4g carb. (3g sugars, 1g fiber), 9g pro.*

"Poultry is pretty amazing because it's versatile. It yields delicious flavor with both moist and dry heat."

CHEESE & RED PEPPER LATKES

SERVES 12

PREP: 30 MIN. COOK: 5 MIN./BATCH

- 3 large onions, finely chopped
- 3 medium sweet red peppers, finely chopped
- ⅓ cup butter, cubed
- 18 medium garlic cloves, minced, divided
- 1 Tbsp. celery salt
- 1 Tbsp. coarsely ground pepper
- 3 lbs. russet potatoes, peeled and shredded
- 1½ cups grated Parmesan cheese
- 1½ cups shredded cheddar cheese
- 1 cup shredded part-skim mozzarella cheese
- 1 cup all-purpose flour
- ¾ cup sour cream
- Canola oil for frying
- Minced fresh parsley

In the Titan Pan, saute onions and red peppers in butter until tender. Add ¼ cup garlic, celery salt and pepper; cook 1 minute longer.

Transfer to a large bowl. Add the potatoes, cheeses, flour, sour cream and remaining garlic; mix well.

Heat ¼ in. oil in pan over medium heat. Working in batches, drop batter by ¼ cupfuls into hot oil. Press lightly to flatten. Fry until golden brown, carefully turning once. Drain on paper towels. Sprinkle with minced parsley.

3 POTATO PANCAKES *437 cal., 29g fat (11g sat. fat), 46mg chol., 677mg sod., 33g carb. (5g sugars, 3g fiber), 12g pro.*

HARVEST PUMPKIN PANCAKES

SERVES 4
TAKES: 30 MIN.

- 1 Tbsp. butter
- 1 large tart apple, peeled and thinly sliced
- 2 Tbsp. brown sugar
- 2 Tbsp. maple syrup
- ½ tsp. ground cinnamon

PANCAKES

- 1 cup all-purpose flour
- 1 Tbsp. sugar
- 1½ tsp. baking powder
- 1½ tsp. pumpkin pie spice
- ½ tsp. salt
- 2 large eggs
- 1 cup 2% milk
- ⅓ cup canned pumpkin
- 2 Tbsp. canola oil
- ½ cup chopped walnuts, toasted

In the Titan Pan, heat butter over medium-high heat. Add apple; cook and stir 3-4 minutes or until tender. Stir in brown sugar, maple syrup and cinnamon; cook and stir 1 minute longer. Remove from heat; keep warm.

For pancakes, in a large bowl, whisk flour, sugar, baking powder, pie spice and salt. In another bowl, whisk the eggs, milk, pumpkin and oil until blended. Add to flour mixture; stir just until moistened. Stir in walnuts.

Lightly grease the pan; heat over medium heat. Pour batter by scant ⅓ cupfuls into pan. Cook until bubbles on top begin to pop and bottoms are golden brown. Turn; cook until second side is golden brown. Serve with apple topping.

Freeze option Prepare pancakes only. Freeze cooled pancakes between layers of waxed paper in a freezer container. To use, place pancakes in an ungreased Titan Pan, cover and reheat in a preheated 350° oven for 5-10 minutes. Meanwhile, prepare apple topping as directed; serve with pancakes.

2 PANCAKES WITH ¼ CUP TOPPING *459 cal., 24g fat (5g sat. fat), 106mg chol., 537mg sod., 54g carb. (25g sugars, 3g fiber), 11g pro.*

CHEF TIP

So that everyone can enjoy breakfast at once, place cooked pancakes from early batches on a wire rack set on a baking sheet in a 200° oven until the last batch is done.

EGGS IN PURGATORY

SERVES 4
TAKES: 30 MIN.

- 2 Tbsp. canola oil
- 1 medium onion, chopped
- ¼ cup tomato paste
- 2 garlic cloves, minced
- 2 tsp. smoked paprika
- ½ tsp. sugar
- ½ tsp. crushed red pepper flakes
- 2 cans (14½ oz. each) fire-roasted diced tomatoes, undrained
- 4 large eggs
- ¼ cup shredded Manchego or Monterey Jack cheese
- 2 Tbsp. minced fresh parsley
- 1 tube (18 oz.) polenta, sliced and warmed, optional

In the Titan Pan, heat oil over medium-high heat. Add onion; cook and stir 6-8 minutes or until tender. Stir in tomato paste, garlic, paprika, sugar and pepper flakes; cook 2 minutes longer.

Stir in tomatoes; bring to a boil. Reduce heat to maintain a simmer. With the back of a spoon, make 4 wells in sauce. Break an egg into each well. Sprinkle with cheese; cook, covered, 8-10 minutes or until egg whites are completely set and yolks begin to thicken but are not hard. Sprinkle with parsley. If desired, serve with polenta.

1 SERVING *255 cal., 14g fat (4g sat. fat), 193mg chol., 676mg sod., 20g carb. (9g sugars, 3g fiber), 11g pro.*

HEALTH TIP

Vitamins A and C are an important part of the immune system, so the tomatoes in this dish will help keep you healthy and energized.

TOAD IN THE HOLE BACON SANDWICH

SERVES 1
TAKES: 15 MIN.

- 2 slices sourdough bread
- 1 Tbsp. mayonnaise
- 1 large egg
- 1 slice cheddar cheese
- 2 cooked bacon strips

Using a biscuit cutter or round cookie cutter, cut out center of 1 slice of bread (discard center or save for another use). Spread mayonnaise on 1 side of bread slices. In the Titan Pan, lightly toast cutout slice, mayonnaise side down, over medium-low heat. Flip slice; crack an egg into center. Add remaining bread slice, mayonnaise side down, to pan; layer with cheese and bacon.

Cook, covered, until egg white is set, yolk is soft-set and cheese begins to melt. If needed, flip slice with egg to finish cooking. To assemble sandwich, use solid slice as bottom and the cutout slice as top.

1 SANDWICH *610 cal., 34g fat (11g sat. fat), 240mg chol., 1220mg sod., 46g carb. (4g sugars, 2g fiber), 30g pro.*

"You can spend your entire life mastering eggs and breakfast and it would be a life well spent."

BACON-CHEESE BURGER BALLS

SERVES 18
PREP: 25 MIN. COOK: 10 MIN.

- 3 large eggs, divided use
- 1 envelope onion soup mix
- 1 lb. ground beef
- 2 Tbsp. all-purpose flour
- 2 Tbsp. 2% milk
- 1 cup shredded cheddar cheese
- 4 bacon strips, cooked and crumbled
- 1 cup crushed saltines (about 30 crackers)
- 5 Tbsp. canola oil

In a large bowl, combine 1 egg and soup mix. Crumble beef over mixture and mix well. Divide into 36 portions; set aside. In another large bowl, combine the flour and milk until smooth. Add cheese and bacon; mix well.

Shape cheese mixture into 36 balls. Shape 1 beef portion around each cheese ball. In a shallow bowl, beat remaining 2 eggs. Place cracker crumbs in another bowl. Dip meatballs into eggs, then coat with crumbs.

Heat oil in the Titan Pan over medium heat. Cook meatballs until meat is no longer pink and coating is golden brown, 10-12 minutes.

2 MEATBALLS *151 cal., 11g fat (3g sat. fat), 55mg chol., 274mg sod., 5g carb. (0 sugars, 0 fiber), 8g pro.*

TOUCHDOWN BRAT SLIDERS

SERVES 16
TAKES: 50 MIN.

- 5 thick-sliced bacon strips, chopped
- 1 lb. uncooked bratwurst links, casings removed
- 1 large onion, finely chopped
- 2 garlic cloves, minced
- 1 pkg. (8 oz.) cream cheese, cubed
- 1 cup dark beer or nonalcoholic beer
- 1 Tbsp. Dijon mustard
- ¼ tsp. pepper
- 16 dinner rolls, split and toasted
- 2 cups cheddar and sour cream potato chips, crushed

In the Titan Pan, cook bacon over medium heat until crisp. Remove to paper towels with a slotted spoon; drain, reserving drippings. Cook bratwurst and onion in drippings over medium heat, breaking into crumbles until meat is no longer pink. Add garlic; cook 1 minute longer. Drain well.

Stir in the cream cheese, beer, mustard and pepper. Bring to a boil. Reduce heat; simmer, uncovered, until thickened, 15-20 minutes, stirring occasionally. Stir in bacon. Spoon ¼ cup onto each roll; sprinkle with chips. Replace tops.

1 SLIDER *354 cal., 24g fat (10g sat. fat), 62mg chol., 617mg sod., 23g carb. (2g sugars, 2g fiber), 10g pro.*

CHOP, CHOP!

To quickly chop an onion, peel it and cut it in half from the root to the top. Leaving the root attached, place each half flat side down on the work surface. Cut vertically through the onion, leaving the root end uncut. Cut across the onion, discarding root end. The closer the cuts, the more finely the onion will be chopped.

MINI ROSEMARY-ROAST BEEF SANDWICHES

SERVES 24

PREP: 25 MIN. + CHILLING BAKE: 50 MIN. + CHILLING

- 1 beef top round roast (3 lbs.)
- 3 tsp. kosher salt
- 2 tsp. crushed dried rosemary
- 2 Tbsp. olive oil, divided
- 2 tsp. pepper
- 2 cups mild giardiniera, drained
- 1 cup reduced-fat mayonnaise
- 2 Tbsp. stone-ground mustard
- 1 to 2 Tbsp. prepared horseradish
- 24 Hawaiian sweet rolls, split

Sprinkle roast with salt and rosemary; wrap tightly in plastic. Refrigerate at least 8 hours or up to 24 hours.

Preheat oven to 325°. Unwrap roast and pat dry. Rub roast with 1 Tbsp. oil; sprinkle with pepper. In the Titan Pan, heat remaining oil over medium-high heat. Brown roast on both sides.

Transfer to oven; roast until a thermometer reads 135° for medium-rare, 50-60 minutes. (Temperature of the roast will continue to rise about 10° upon standing.) Remove roast from pan; let stand 1 hour. Refrigerate, covered, at least 2 hours, until cold.

Place giardiniera in a food processor; pulse until finely chopped. In a small bowl, mix mayonnaise, mustard and horseradish.

To serve, thinly slice cold beef. Serve on rolls with mayonnaise mixture and giardiniera.

1 MINI SANDWICH *220 cal., 9g fat (3g sat. fat), 50mg chol., 466mg sod., 18g carb. (7g sugars, 1g fiber), 17g pro.*

BUTTERNUT-GOUDA POT STICKERS

BUTTERNUT-GOUDA POT STICKERS

SERVES 12
PREP: 45 MIN. COOK: 15 MIN.

- 1 small butternut squash (about 2½ lbs.), peeled and cubed
- 1 Tbsp. butter
- 1 small sweet red pepper, finely chopped
- 1 small onion, finely chopped
- 2 cups shredded Gouda cheese
- ½ tsp. salt
- ½ tsp. minced fresh thyme or ⅛ tsp. dried thyme
- ½ tsp. pepper
- 1 pkg. (10 oz.) pot sticker or gyoza wrappers
- 3 Tbsp. canola oil, divided
- ¾ cup water, divided

Place squash in the Titan Pan and add enough water to cover. Bring to a boil over medium-high heat; reduce heat and simmer, covered, until soft, 10-15 minutes. Drain. Remove squash to a separate bowl; mash.

In same pan, heat butter over medium heat; saute pepper and onion until tender, 4-6 minutes. Add to squash; stir in cheese, salt, thyme and pepper.

Place 1 Tbsp. filling on each wrapper (keep the remaining wrappers covered with a damp towel). Moisten edge of wrapper with water; fold over to enclose filling, while pleating the front side to form a pouch. Stand pot sticker on a work surface to flatten bottom, curving ends slightly.

In the Titan Pan, heat 1 Tbsp. oil over medium heat. Place a third of the pot stickers in pan; cook until bottoms are lightly browned, 1-2 minutes. Add ¼ cup water (water may spatter); cook, covered, until filling is heated through, 3-4 minutes. Uncover; cook until bottoms are crisp and water is evaporated, 1-2 minutes. Repeat twice.

Freeze option Cover and freeze uncooked pot stickers on lightly floured baking sheets until firm. Transfer to airtight freezer containers; return to freezer. To use, cook pot stickers as directed, increasing time as necessary to heat through.

4 POT STICKERS *220 cal., 10g fat (4g sat. fat), 26mg chol., 336mg sod., 27g carb. (4g sugars, 4g fiber), 8g pro.*

YOGURT-HUMMUS CHIPS WITH LAMB

SERVES 6
TAKES: 30 MIN.

- ½ lb. ground lamb or lean ground beef (90% lean)
- 1 Tbsp. pine nuts
- ¼ tsp. salt
- ⅛ tsp. pepper
- 6 Tbsp. plain yogurt, divided
- 1 pkg. (7.33 oz.) baked pita chips
- 1 cup prepared tabbouleh
- ½ cup hummus
- 1 large tomato, chopped
- ¼ cup sliced ripe olives
- 1 Tbsp. minced fresh parsley
- 1 Tbsp. minced fresh mint
- Chopped red onion, optional

In the Titan Pan, cook lamb over medium heat until no longer pink, breaking into crumbles, 4-6 minutes; drain. Stir in pine nuts, salt and pepper; cool slightly. Stir in 2 Tbsp. yogurt.

Arrange pita chips on a serving platter. Layer with lamb mixture, tabbouleh, hummus, tomato, olives, parsley, mint, remaining yogurt and, if desired, onion. Serve immediately.

1 SERVING *299 cal., 14g fat (4g sat. fat), 27mg chol., 624mg sod., 29g carb. (2g sugars, 4g fiber), 13g pro.*

HOME GROUND

Experience the incredible flavor of beef you've ground yourself: Freeze 1 lb. chuck roast for 15 minutes. Cut the frozen meat into small cubes. • Place the cubes in a food processor. Pulse 20 to 22 times until the meat is coarsely ground.

CINNAMON-APPLE PORK CHOPS

SERVES 4

TAKES: 25 MIN.

- 2 Tbsp. reduced-fat butter, divided
- 4 boneless pork loin chops (4 oz. each)
- 3 Tbsp. brown sugar
- 1 tsp. ground cinnamon
- ½ tsp. ground nutmeg
- ¼ tsp. salt
- 4 medium tart apples, thinly sliced
- 2 Tbsp. chopped pecans

In the Titan Pan, heat 1 Tbsp. butter over medium heat. Add pork chops; cook 4-5 minutes on each side or until a thermometer reads 145°. Meanwhile, in a small bowl, mix brown sugar, cinnamon, nutmeg and salt.

Remove chops; keep warm. Add apples, pecans, sugar mixture and remaining 1 Tbsp. butter to pan; cook and stir until apples are tender. Serve with chops.

1 PORK CHOP WITH ⅔ CUP APPLE MIXTURE *316 cal., 12g fat (4g sat. fat), 62mg chol., 232mg sod., 31g carb. (25g sugars, 4g fiber), 22g pro.*

TURKEY SCALLOPINI MARSALA

SERVES 4
TAKES: 30 MIN.

- ½ cup all-purpose flour
- ½ tsp. salt
- ½ tsp. pepper
- 1 pkg. (17.6 oz.) turkey breast cutlets
- 2 Tbsp. olive oil
- 1½ cups Marsala wine
- 3 Tbsp. butter
- 3 Tbsp. shredded Parmesan cheese
- Hot cooked linguine, optional

In a shallow dish, mix flour, salt and pepper. Dredge turkey cutlets in flour mixture.

In the Titan Pan, heat oil over medium heat. Add turkey; cook 3-4 minutes on each side or until meat is no longer pink. Remove from pan. Stir in wine. Bring to a boil; cook 8-10 minutes or until liquid is reduced to about ½ cup. Stir in butter until melted. Return turkey to pan; heat through. Serve with cheese and, if desired, linguine.

1 SERVING *459 cal., 17g fat (7g sat. fat), 103mg chol., 341mg sod., 18g carb. (7g sugars, 0 fiber), 33g pro.*

BARBECUED PORK & PENNE

BARBECUED PORK & PENNE

SERVES 8
TAKES: 25 MIN.

- 1 pkg. (16 oz.) penne pasta
- 1 cup chopped sweet red pepper
- ¾ cup chopped onion
- 1 Tbsp. butter
- 1 Tbsp. olive oil
- 3 garlic cloves, minced
- 1 carton (16 oz.) refrigerated fully cooked barbecued shredded pork
- 1 can (14½ oz.) diced tomatoes with mild green chiles, undrained
- ½ cup beef broth
- 1 tsp. ground cumin
- 1 tsp. pepper
- ¼ tsp. salt
- 1¼ cups shredded cheddar cheese
- ¼ cup chopped green onions

Cook pasta according to the package directions. Meanwhile, in the Titan Pan, saute red pepper and onion in butter and oil until tender. Add garlic; saute 1 minute longer. Stir in the pork, tomatoes, broth, cumin, pepper and salt; heat through.

Drain pasta. Add pasta and cheese to pork mixture; stir until blended. Sprinkle with green onions.

Freeze option Freeze cooled pasta mixture in freezer containers. To use, partially thaw in refrigerator overnight. Simmer over medium-low heat in the Titan Pan until heated through.

1¼ CUPS *428 cal., 11g fat (6g sat. fat), 40mg chol., 903mg sod., 61g carb. (16g sugars, 4g fiber), 20g pro.*

CHEF TIP

You can freeze cooled pasta in freezer containers. To use, partially thaw in the refrigerator overnight. When you're ready to eat, toss the pasta into your Titan Pan and heat the dish to your desired temperature.

PISTACHIO SALMON WITH VEGGIES

SERVES 4
PREP: 35 MIN. BAKE: 10 MIN.

- ½ cup onion and garlic salad croutons
- ½ cup pistachios
- 1 large egg white
- 2 Tbsp. water
- 4 salmon fillets (6 oz. each), about 1 in. thick
- 4 oz. reduced-fat cream cheese
- 2 Tbsp. lemon juice
- 2 Tbsp. snipped fresh dill
- 1 Tbsp. capers, drained
- 2 Tbsp. olive oil, divided
- 1½ cups julienned fresh carrots
- 1½ cups julienned yellow summer squash
- 1½ cups julienned sweet red pepper
- ½ tsp. salt
- ¼ cup radishes, halved and finely sliced
- Lemon wedges, optional

Pulse croutons and pistachios in a food processor until finely chopped. Whisk egg white with water. Pat salmon fillets dry; dip in egg white, then roll in crouton-pistachio mixture. Refrigerate 30 minutes. Meanwhile, combine cream cheese, lemon juice, dill and capers until well blended.

Preheat oven to 350°. In the Titan Pan, heat 1 Tbsp. oil over medium-high heat. Add carrots, squash, red pepper and salt; cook and stir until tender and lightly caramelized, 6-8 minutes. Remove.

In the same pan, heat remaining oil over medium heat. Add salmon; cook 1 minute on each side until golden brown. Place pan in oven; bake until fish just begins to flake easily with a fork, 8-10 minutes. Serve vegetables with salmon; top with sauce. Sprinkle with radishes. If desired, serve with lemon wedges.

1 FILLET WITH 3 TBSP. SAUCE AND ¾ CUP VEGETABLES
550 cal., 37g fat (9g sat. fat), 106mg chol., 722mg sod., 18g carb. (8g sugars, 4g fiber), 38g pro.

HEALTH TIP

Save leftover pistachios for snacking! One serving (about 50 nuts) has 6g protein, 3g fiber and more than 10% of the daily value for B6, thiamin, copper and phosphorous.

PISTACHIO SALMON WITH VEGGIES

PEANUT BUTTER PORK CURRY

PEANUT BUTTER PORK CURRY

SERVES 4

PREP: 15 MIN. COOK: 20 MIN.

- 2 pork tenderloins (¾ lb. each), cubed
- 1 tsp. salt, divided
- ½ tsp. pepper
- 1 Tbsp. olive oil
- 1 cup sliced fresh carrots
- 1 medium onion, chopped
- 2 garlic cloves, minced
- 1 can (14½ oz.) diced tomatoes, drained
- 1 cup chicken broth
- 1 cup cream of coconut or coconut milk
- ½ cup creamy peanut butter
- 3 tsp. curry powder
- ¼ tsp. cayenne pepper
- Cooked brown rice

Sprinkle pork with ½ tsp. salt and the pepper. In the Titan Pan, heat oil over medium-high heat. Add the pork; cook and stir until no longer pink, 4-6 minutes. Remove from the pan.

In same pan, cook carrots and onion until softened, 4-6 minutes. Add garlic; cook 2 minutes. Return pork to pan. Add tomatoes and broth. Reduce heat; simmer, covered, 6-8 minutes.

Stir in cream of coconut, peanut butter, curry, cayenne and remaining ½ tsp. salt until smooth. Simmer, uncovered, until thickened slightly, about 2 minutes. Serve with brown rice.

1 CUP *463 cal., 24g fat (9g sat. fat), 64mg chol., 837mg sod., 36g carb. (29g sugars, 4g fiber), 29g pro.*

STOVETOP MACARONI & CHEESE

SERVES 6
TAKES: 25 MIN.

- 1 pkg. (7 oz.) elbow macaroni
- ¼ cup butter, cubed
- ¼ cup all-purpose flour
- ½ tsp. salt
- Dash pepper
- 2 cups whole milk
- 8 oz. sharp cheddar cheese, shredded
- Paprika, optional

Cook macaroni in the Titan Pan according to package directions. Drain and set aside.

In the pan, melt butter over medium heat. Stir in flour, salt and pepper until smooth; gradually whisk in milk. Bring to a boil, stirring constantly; cook and stir 1-2 minutes longer or until thickened. Stir in cheese until melted. Add macaroni; stir to coat and heat through. If desired, sprinkle with paprika.

1 CUP *388 cal., 22g fat (15g sat. fat), 72mg chol., 542mg sod., 33g carb. (5g sugars, 1g fiber), 16g pro.*

STOVETOP MACARONI & CHEESE

MAPLE & BACON GLAZED SPROUTS

SERVES 4
PREP: 15 MIN. COOK: 20 MIN.

- 5 bacon strips, chopped
- 1 lb. fresh Brussels sprouts, trimmed
- 3 Tbsp. butter
- ½ cup chicken broth
- ¼ cup chopped pecans
- ¼ cup maple syrup
- ¼ tsp. salt
- ¼ tsp. pepper

In the Titan Pan, cook bacon over medium heat until crisp. Remove to paper towels with a slotted spoon; drain drippings from pan.

Meanwhile, cut an "X" in the core of each Brussels sprout. In the pan, saute sprouts in butter until lightly browned, 4-5 minutes.

Stir in the broth, pecans, maple syrup, salt and pepper. Bring to a boil. Reduce heat; cover and simmer for 5 minutes. Uncover; cook and stir until sprouts are tender, 8-10 minutes longer. Sprinkle with bacon.

¾ CUP *273 cal., 18g fat (7g sat. fat), 32mg chol., 544mg sod., 25g carb. (15g sugars, 5g fiber), 8g pro.*

CHEF TIP

The boiling of Brussels sprouts has ruined the vegetable for so many. Let's change all of that! Just follow these three tips:

1. Be sure to brown the sprouts and get the leaves crispy.
2. Season generously.
3. Keep them al dente inside so they'll have some texture.

GARLIC POTATOES & PEPPERS

SERVES 8

PREP: 10 MIN. COOK: 35 MIN.

- 2 Tbsp. olive oil
- 12 garlic cloves, peeled
- 2 lbs. potatoes, cut into ¼- to ½-in. cubes (about 7 cups)
- 1 tsp. salt
- ½ tsp. pepper
- 1 large sweet red pepper, cut into ½-in. pieces

In the Titan Pan, heat oil over medium-low heat. Add garlic cloves; cook, uncovered, until almost tender, 10 minutes, stirring occasionally.

Increase heat to medium. Stir in potatoes, salt and pepper. Cook, uncovered, 15 minutes, stirring occasionally. Add red pepper; cook and stir until potatoes are tender, about 10 minutes.

¾ CUP *131 cal., 4g fat (1g sat. fat), 0 chol., 303mg sod., 23g carb. (2g sugars, 3g fiber), 3g pro.*

GARLIC POTATOES & PEPPERS

AUTUMN HARVEST MASHED POTATOES

SERVES 10

PREP: 35 MIN. COOK: 25 MIN.

- 4 large red potatoes, cubed
- 3 medium turnips, cubed
- 2 medium parsnips, peeled and cubed
- ⅓ cup butter, cubed
- 1 can (15 oz.) pumpkin
- 1 tsp. garlic salt with parsley
- ¾ tsp. salt
- ½ tsp. pepper
- ⅛ tsp. ground nutmeg

Place the potatoes, turnips and parsnips in the Titan Pan; cover with water. Bring to a boil. Reduce the heat; cover and simmer for 15-20 minutes or until tender. Drain.

Mash vegetables with butter; stir in the pumpkin, garlic salt, salt, pepper and nutmeg. Transfer to a serving bowl.

¾ CUP *218 cal., 7g fat (4g sat. fat), 16mg chol., 348mg sod., 38g carb. (7g sugars, 6g fiber), 5g pro.*

KALE & FENNEL SAUTE

SERVES 6

PREP: 10 MIN. COOK: 25 MIN.

- 2 Tbsp. extra virgin olive oil
- 1 small onion, thinly sliced
- 1 small fennel bulb, thinly sliced
- ½ lb. fully cooked apple chicken sausage links or cooked Italian sausage links, halved lengthwise and sliced into half-moons
- 2 garlic cloves, minced
- 3 Tbsp. dry sherry or dry white wine
- 1 Tbsp. herbes de Provence
- ⅛ tsp. salt
- ⅛ tsp. pepper
- 1 bunch kale, trimmed and torn into bite-sized pieces

In the Titan Pan, heat olive oil over medium-high heat. Add onion and fennel; cook and stir until onion begins to brown, 6-8 minutes. Add sausage, garlic, sherry and seasonings; cook until sausage starts to caramelize, 4-6 minutes.

Add kale; cook, covered, stirring occasionally, until kale is tender, 15-17 minutes.

¾ CUP *167 cal., 8g fat (2g sat. fat), 27mg chol., 398mg sod., 16g carb. (6g sugars, 3g fiber), 9g pro.*

CHEF TIP

Vegetables usually contain a lot of moisture, so cook them quickly with very high heat. Slow cooking will cause them to get soggy and lose all the delicious properties we want to exploit.

SPICED PINEAPPLE UPSIDE-DOWN CAKE

SERVES 12

PREP: 15 MIN. BAKE: 40 MIN.

- 1⅓ cups butter, softened, divided
- 1 cup packed brown sugar
- 1 can (20 oz.) pineapple slices, drained
- 10 to 12 maraschino cherries
- ½ cup chopped pecans
- 1½ cups sugar
- 2 large eggs, room temperature
- 1 tsp. vanilla extract
- 2 cups all-purpose flour
- 2 tsp. baking powder
- ½ tsp. baking soda
- ½ tsp. salt
- ½ tsp. ground cinnamon
- ½ tsp. ground nutmeg
- 1 cup buttermilk

In the Titan Pan, melt ⅔ cup butter; stir in brown sugar. Arrange pineapple in a single layer over sugar mixture; place a cherry in the center of each slice. Sprinkle with pecans and set aside.

In a large bowl, cream sugar and remaining butter until light and fluffy. Add eggs, 1 at a time, beating well after each addition. Beat in vanilla. Combine flour, baking powder, baking soda, salt, cinnamon and nutmeg; add alternately to batter with the buttermilk, beating well after each addition.

Carefully pour over the pineapple. Bake at 350° until a toothpick inserted in the center comes out clean, about 40 minutes. Immediately invert onto a serving platter. Serve warm.

1 PIECE *509 cal., 25g fat (13g sat. fat), 91mg chol., 467mg sod., 69g carb. (52g sugars, 2g fiber), 5g pro.*

CARAMEL DUMPLINGS

SERVES 8

PREP: 10 MIN. COOK: 30 MIN.

- 2 Tbsp. butter
- 1½ cups packed brown sugar
- 1½ cups water

DUMPLINGS

- 1¼ cups all-purpose flour
- ½ cup sugar
- 2 tsp. baking powder
- ½ tsp. salt
- ½ cup whole milk
- 2 Tbsp. butter, softened
- 2 tsp. vanilla extract
- ½ cup coarsely chopped peeled apple, optional

In the Titan Pan, heat the butter, brown sugar and water to boiling. Reduce heat to simmer.

Meanwhile, combine the dumpling ingredients. Drop by tablespoonfuls into the simmering sauce. Cover tightly and simmer for 20 minutes. Do not lift lid. Serve warm, with cream or ice cream if desired.

½ CUP *336 cal., 6g fat (4g sat. fat), 17mg chol., 329mg sod., 68g carb. (53g sugars, 1g fiber), 3g pro.*

3 WAYS TO SOFTEN BUTTER

Cut butter into cubes and let stand at room temperature about 20 minutes. • Roll out butter between 2 sheets of waxed paper. If you use this method, butter may still be a bit cold, so you'll have to beat butter and sugar longer if a creamed texture is required in your recipe. • Use a cheese grater to shred cold butter. This method works quickly, but cleanup can be messy.

POACHED PEARS WITH ORANGE CREAM

SERVES 2
PREP: 10 MIN. COOK: 45 MIN. + COOLING

- 2 firm medium pears
- 1½ cups water
- 1 cup dry red wine or red grape juice
- ½ cup sugar
- 2 tsp. vanilla extract
- ¼ cup reduced-fat sour cream
- 2 tsp. confectioners' sugar
- ½ tsp. grated orange zest
- ⅛ tsp. orange extract
- Additional grated orange zest, optional

Core pears from bottom, leaving stems intact. Peel pears; cut ¼ in. from bottom to level if necessary. Place pears on their sides in a large saucepan. Add water, wine, sugar and vanilla. Bring to a boil. Reduce heat; simmer, covered, turning once, until pears are almost tender, 35-40 minutes. (For more intense flavor and color, leave fruit in cooking liquid and refrigerate overnight.)

Meanwhile, combine sour cream, confectioners' sugar, orange zest and extract. Refrigerate until serving. Remove pears with a slotted spoon; pat dry and, if warm, cool to room temperature. Discard cooking liquid. Place pears on dessert plates. Serve with orange cream; if desired, top with additional grated orange zest.

1 PEAR WITH ABOUT 2 TBSP. CREAM *239 cal., 3g fat (2g sat. fat), 10mg chol., 23mg sod., 46g carb. (36g sugars, 5g fiber), 3g pro.*

CARAMEL-APPLE SKILLET BUCKLE

SERVES 12

PREP: 35 MIN. BAKE: 1 HOUR + STANDING

- ½ cup butter, softened
- ¾ cup sugar
- 2 large eggs, room temperature
- 1 tsp. vanilla extract
- 2 cups all-purpose flour
- 2½ tsp. baking powder
- 1¾ tsp. ground cinnamon
- ½ tsp. ground ginger
- ¼ tsp. salt
- 1½ cups buttermilk

TOPPING

- ⅔ cup packed brown sugar
- ½ cup all-purpose flour
- ¼ cup cold butter
- ¾ cup finely chopped pecans
- ½ cup old-fashioned oats
- 6 cups thinly sliced peeled Gala or other sweet apples (about 6 medium)
- 18 caramels, unwrapped
- 1 Tbsp. buttermilk
- Optional: Whipped cream or ice cream, chopped pecans, ground cinnamon

Preheat oven to 350°. In a large bowl, cream butter and sugar until light and fluffy, 5-7 minutes. Add eggs, 1 at a time, beating well after each addition. Beat in vanilla. In another bowl, whisk the flour, baking powder, cinnamon, ginger and salt; add to creamed mixture alternately with buttermilk, beating well after each addition. Pour into a lightly greased Titan Pan.

For topping, in a small bowl, mix brown sugar and flour; cut in butter until crumbly. Stir in pecans and oats; sprinkle over batter. Top with apples. Bake until apples are golden brown, 60-70 minutes. Cool in pan on a wire rack.

In a microwave, melt caramels with buttermilk; stir until smooth. Drizzle over cake. Let stand until set. If desired, top with whipped cream or ice cream, chopped pecans and a sprinkling of cinnamon.

1 SLICE *462 cal., 19g fat (9g sat. fat), 64mg chol., 354mg sod., 68g carb. (42g sugars, 3g fiber), 7g pro.*

FAVORITE CHOCOLATE-BOURBON PECAN TART

SERVES 12

PREP: 15 MIN. BAKE: 30 MIN. + COOLING

Pastry for single-crust pie
½ cup semisweet chocolate chips
2 large eggs, room temperature
¾ cup dark corn syrup
½ cup sugar
¼ cup butter, melted
2 Tbsp. bourbon
¼ tsp. salt
1 cup pecan halves, toasted
¼ cup hot caramel ice cream topping

Preheat the oven to 375°. On a lightly floured surface, roll dough to a 12-in. circle. Press onto bottom and partway up the sides of the Titan Pan. Sprinkle with chocolate chips.

Beat eggs, corn syrup, sugar, butter, bourbon and salt. Stir in pecans. Pour over chocolate chips. Bake until center is just set and crust is golden brown, 30-35 minutes.

Cool on a wire rack. Cut into slices. Serve with caramel topping.

1 SLICE *357 cal., 20g fat (9g sat. fat), 61mg chol., 250mg sod., 43g carb. (32g sugars, 2g fiber), 4g pro.*

PASTRY FOR SINGLE-CRUST PIE

Combine 1¼ cups all-purpose flour and ¼ tsp. salt; cut in ½ cup cold butter until crumbly. Gradually add 3-5 Tbsp. ice water, tossing with a fork until the dough holds together when pressed. Cover and refrigerate 1 hour.

CHAPTER 4

WINTER

PECAN-OATMEAL PANCAKES

PECAN-OATMEAL PANCAKES

SERVES 5
TAKES: 30 MIN.

- 1½ cups quick-cooking oats
- 1 cup all-purpose flour
- 2 Tbsp. brown sugar
- 2 tsp. baking powder
- ¼ tsp. salt
- 1½ cups whole milk
- 2 large eggs, lightly beaten
- 2 Tbsp. butter or margarine, melted
- ½ cup chopped pecans

In a bowl, combine the oats, flour, brown sugar, baking powder and salt. Combine milk, eggs and butter; stir into dry ingredients just until blended. Fold in pecans. Pour batter by ¼ cupfuls into a greased Titan Pan over medium-high heat; turn when bubbles form on top of pancakes. Cook until second side is golden brown.

3 PANCAKES *402 cal., 19g fat (6g sat. fat), 107mg chol., 389mg sod., 45g carb. (10g sugars, 4g fiber), 12g pro.*

CHEF TIP

Ease rushed mornings by getting a head start on breakfast. For pancakes, combine the wet ingredients and refrigerate overnight. Combine the dry ingredients, cover and store on the counter.

SAVORY BREAKFAST CASSEROLE

SERVES 12

PREP: 20 MIN. BAKE: 25 MIN.

- 1 lb. bulk Italian sausage
- 1 cup chopped onion
- 1 jar (7 oz.) roasted red peppers, drained and chopped, divided
- 1 pkg. (10 oz.) frozen chopped spinach, thawed and well drained
- 1 cup all-purpose flour
- ¼ cup grated Parmesan cheese
- 1 tsp. dried basil
- ½ tsp. salt
- 8 large eggs
- 2 cups whole milk
- 1 cup shredded provolone cheese
- Fresh rosemary sprigs, optional

Preheat oven to 425°. In the Titan Pan, cook sausage and onion over medium heat until sausage is no longer pink; drain. Sprinkle half the red peppers and all the spinach over the sausage mixture.

In a bowl, combine flour, Parmesan cheese, basil and salt. Combine eggs and milk; add to dry ingredients and mix well. Pour over spinach.

Bake 20-25 minutes or until a knife inserted in the center comes out clean. Sprinkle with provolone cheese and remaining red peppers. Bake 2 minutes longer or until cheese is melted. Let stand 5 minutes before cutting. Garnish with rosemary if desired.

1 SERVING *232 cal., 13g fat (6g sat. fat), 170mg chol., 531mg sod., 13g carb. (4g sugars, 1g fiber), 14g pro.*

> “When you have no idea what to cook, if you have eggs, you're halfway to a meal.”

BACON ROLL-UPS

BACON ROLL-UPS

SERVES 5

PREP: 25 MIN. COOK: 20 MIN.

- ⅓ cup finely chopped onion
- 1 Tbsp. butter
- 3 cups cubed day-old bread
- ¼ tsp. celery salt
- ¼ tsp. garlic powder
- ⅛ tsp. salt
- ⅛ tsp. pepper
- 1 large egg, lightly beaten
- 10 bacon strips

In the Titan Pan, saute onion in butter until tender. In a large bowl, combine the bread cubes, celery salt, garlic powder, salt, pepper and onion mixture; toss to mix evenly. Add egg; toss to coat bread cubes. Roll into ten 1¼-in. balls. Wrap a bacon strip around each ball and secure with a toothpick.

In the Titan Pan, cook bacon roll-ups on all sides over medium heat for 18 minutes or until bacon is crisp and a thermometer inserted into stuffing reads at least 160°. Drain on paper towels.

2 ROLL-UPS *348 cal., 30g fat (11g sat. fat), 79mg chol., 613mg sod., 12g carb. (2g sugars, 1g fiber), 7g pro.*

DAYBREAK TACOS

SERVES 8
TAKES: 25 MIN.

- ⅓ cup black beans, rinsed and drained
- ⅓ cup cubed avocado
- ⅓ cup pico de gallo
- 1 Tbsp. lime juice
- 1 cup frozen O'Brien potatoes, thawed
- ½ lb. bulk pork sausage
- 6 large eggs
- 2 Tbsp. 2% milk
- ½ cup shredded Monterey Jack cheese
- 8 flour tortillas (6 in.), warmed
- Optional: Sour cream, fresh chopped cilantro and additional pico de gallo

Gently mix black beans, avocado, pico de gallo and lime juice; set aside. In the Titan Pan, cook potatoes and crumble sausage over medium heat until sausage is no longer pink and potatoes are tender, 6-8 minutes.

Whisk together eggs and milk. Pour into pan; cook and stir over medium heat until eggs are thickened and no liquid egg remains. Stir in cheese. Spoon egg mixture into tortillas; top with black bean mixture. If desired, serve with sour cream, cilantro and additional pico de gallo.

1 TACO *291 cal., 16g fat (6g sat. fat), 161mg chol., 494mg sod., 22g carb. (1g sugars, 3g fiber), 13g pro.*

PEEL AN AVOCADO IN 4 STEPS

Wash the avocado. Cut into the ripe avocado stem to stern until you hit the pit. Repeat to cut the avocado into quarters. • Twist to separate. • Pull out the pit. • Pull the skin back like a banana peel. Pretty cool, right? Slice or chop as you like.

UPSIDE-DOWN BACON PANCAKE

SERVES 6

PREP: 5 MIN. COOK: 25 MIN. + COOLING

- 6 bacon strips, coarsely chopped
- ¼ cup packed brown sugar
- 2 cups complete buttermilk pancake mix
- 1½ cups water
- Optional: Maple syrup and butter

In the Titan Pan, cook bacon over medium heat until crisp. Remove bacon to paper towels with a slotted spoon. Remove drippings, reserving 2 Tbsp. Return bacon to pan with reserved drippings; sprinkle with brown sugar.

In a small bowl, combine pancake mix and water just until moistened. Pour into pan.

Bake at 350° until a toothpick inserted in the center comes out clean, 18-20 minutes. Cool for 10 minutes before inverting onto a serving plate. Serve warm, with maple syrup and butter if desired.

1 SLICE *265 cal., 9g fat (3g sat. fat), 12mg chol., 802mg sod., 41g carb. (13g sugars, 1g fiber), 6g pro.*

SPICY MIXED NUTS

SERVES 12

PREP: 5 MIN. COOK: 10 MIN. + COOLING

- 3 Tbsp. butter
- 1 can (15 to 16 oz.) mixed nuts
- ¼ tsp. Worcestershire sauce
- ½ tsp. salt
- ¼ tsp. paprika
- ¼ tsp. cayenne pepper
- ¼ tsp. chili powder
- ⅛ tsp. ground cumin

In the Titan Pan, melt butter over low heat. Add nuts and Worcestershire sauce; cook and stir 5-7 minutes. Drain on paper towels. Place nuts in a large bowl. Combine remaining ingredients; sprinkle over nuts, tossing to coat. Cool. Store in an airtight container at room temperature.

¼ CUP *225 cal., 19g fat (2g sat. fat), 0 chol., 232mg sod., 10g carb. (2g sugars, 3g fiber), 7g pro.*

POLYNESIAN MEATBALLS

SERVES 18

PREP: 30 MIN. COOK: 15 MIN.

- 1 can (5 oz.) evaporated milk
- ⅓ cup chopped onion
- ⅔ cup crushed saltines
- 1 tsp. seasoned salt
- 1½ lbs. lean ground beef

SAUCE

- 1 can (20 oz.) pineapple tidbits
- 2 Tbsp. cornstarch
- ½ cup cider vinegar
- 2 Tbsp. soy sauce
- 2 Tbsp. lemon juice
- ½ cup packed brown sugar

In a bowl, combine the milk, onion, saltines and seasoned salt. Crumble beef over mixture and mix well. With wet hands, shape into 1-in. balls. In the Titan Pan over medium heat, brown meatballs in small batches, turning often. Remove with a slotted spoon and keep warm. Drain pan.

Drain pineapple, reserving juice; set pineapple aside. Add enough water to juice to measure 1 cup. In a bowl, combine the cornstarch, pineapple juice mixture, vinegar, soy sauce, lemon juice and brown sugar until smooth. Add to pan. Bring to a boil; cook and stir until thickened, about 2 minutes. Add meatballs. Reduce heat; cover and simmer for 15 minutes. Add the pineapple; heat through.

4 MEATBALLS *150 cal., 5g fat (2g sat. fat), 36mg chol., 244mg sod., 14g carb. (11g sugars, 0 fiber), 11g pro.*

"When making homemade meatballs, ask butchers at the supermarket for a larger grind. The meatballs will feel meatier and taste more delicious."

BACON-WRAPPED PORK MEDALLIONS

SERVES 8

PREP: 20 MIN. BAKE: 15 MIN.

- 16 bacon strips
- 1 pork tenderloin (1 lb.), cut into 8 slices
- Dash garlic powder
- Dash pepper
- 2 large tomatoes, chopped
- 1 cup diced onion

In the Titan Pan, cook bacon over medium heat until partially cooked but not crisp. Remove to paper towels to drain; wipe pan clean and set aside. Flatten pork to ½-in. thickness. Position 2 bacon strips to make an "X"; top with a tenderloin slice. Sprinkle with garlic powder and pepper. Repeat.

Combine tomatoes and onion; spoon over tenderloin. Fold bacon over the top and secure with toothpicks; place in pan. Bake at 350° until a thermometer reads 145°, 15-20 minutes.

1 PIECE *164 cal., 8g fat (3g sat. fat), 48mg chol., 317mg sod., 4g carb. (2g sugars, 1g fiber), 18g pro.*

WARM CRAB & SPINACH DIP

SERVES 18

PREP: 20 MIN. COOK: 15 MIN.

- 2 Tbsp. olive oil
- ⅓ cup finely chopped sweet onion
- 2 garlic cloves, minced
- 1 pkg. (8 oz.) softened cream cheese, cubed
- 1 pkg. (5.2 oz.) Boursin garlic and fine herbs cheese
- ¼ cup 2% milk
- ¼ cup half-and-half cream
- ¼ cup white wine or chicken broth
- 1 Tbsp. seafood seasoning
- 2 tsp. Worcestershire sauce
- 1 tsp. Louisiana-style hot sauce
- ⅛ tsp. crushed red pepper flakes, optional
- 2 cans (6 oz. each) lump crabmeat, drained and picked over
- 1 pkg. (10 oz.) frozen chopped spinach, thawed and squeezed dry
- 2 cups shredded cheddar cheese
- Blue tortilla chips

In the Titan Pan, heat oil over medium heat. Add onion and garlic; cook 3 minutes. Stir in cream cheese and Boursin until melted. Add milk, cream and wine, stirring constantly.

Add seafood seasoning, Worcestershire, hot sauce and, if desired, red pepper flakes. Stir in crab, spinach and cheddar cheese until cheese melts and mixture is bubbly. Serve warm with tortilla chips.

¼ CUP *170 cal., 14g fat (8g sat. fat), 55mg chol., 421mg sod., 2g carb. (1g sugars, 1g fiber), 9g pro.*

WHISKEY-BACON JAM

SERVES 24

PREP: 15 MIN. COOK: 1 HOUR

- 1½ lbs. thick-sliced bacon strips, finely chopped
- 8 shallots, finely chopped
- 1 large sweet onion, finely chopped
- 2 garlic cloves, minced
- 1 tsp. chili powder
- ½ tsp. paprika
- ¼ tsp. kosher salt
- ¼ tsp. pepper
- ½ cup whiskey
- ½ cup maple syrup
- ¼ cup balsamic vinegar
- ½ cup packed brown sugar
- Assorted crackers

In the Titan Pan, cook bacon over medium heat until crisp. Drain on paper towels. Discard all but 2 Tbsp. drippings. Add shallots and onion to the drippings; cook over medium-low heat until caramelized, 30-40 minutes, stirring occasionally.

Stir in garlic; cook 30 seconds. Add seasonings. Remove from heat; stir in whiskey and maple syrup. Increase heat to high; bring to a boil and cook 3 minutes, stirring constantly. Add vinegar and brown sugar; cook another 3 minutes, continuing to stir constantly.

Add bacon pieces; reduce heat to low and cook 12 minutes, stirring every few minutes. Allow jam to cool slightly. Pulse half he jam in a food processor until smooth; stir puree into remaining jam. Serve with assorted crackers.

2 TBSP. *112 cal., 8g fat (3g sat. fat), 10mg chol., 118mg sod., 7g carb. (5g sugars, 0 fiber), 2g pro.*

CHEF TIP

This savory jam lasts only a week in the fridge, so freeze small amounts for a quick snack with crackers.

DEEP-DISH SAUSAGE PIZZA

SERVES 8

PREP: 30 MIN. + RISING BAKE: 30 MIN. + STANDING

- 1 pkg. (¼ oz.) active dry yeast
- ⅔ cup warm water (110° to 115°)
- 1¾ to 2 cups all-purpose flour
- ¼ cup vegetable oil
- 1 tsp. each dried oregano, basil and marjoram
- ½ tsp. garlic salt
- ½ tsp. onion salt

TOPPINGS

- 2 medium green peppers, chopped
- 1 large onion, chopped
- ½ tsp. each dried oregano, basil and marjoram
- 1 Tbsp. olive oil
- 4 cups shredded part-skim mozzarella cheese, divided
- 1 cup grated Parmesan cheese
- 1 lb. bulk pork sausage, cooked and drained
- 1 can (28 oz.) diced tomatoes, well drained
- 2 oz. sliced pepperoni

In a large bowl, dissolve yeast in warm water. Add 1 cup flour, oil and the crust seasonings; beat until smooth. Add enough remaining flour to form a soft dough. Turn onto a floured surface; knead until smooth and elastic, 6-8 minutes. Place in a greased bowl; turn once to grease top. Cover and let rise in a warm place until doubled, about 1 hour.

Meanwhile, in the Titan Pan, saute the green peppers, onion and topping seasonings in oil until tender. Drain and set aside to cool.

Preheat oven to 400°. Punch dough down; roll out into a 15-in. circle. Transfer to the Titan Pan, letting dough climb sides. Sprinkle with 1 cup mozzarella. Layer half the onion mixture over the mozzarella. Layer with half of the Parmesan, sausage and tomatoes. Sprinkle with 2 cups mozzarella. Repeat layering of onion mixture, Parmesan, sausage and tomatoes. Fold crust over to form an edge.

Bake 20 minutes. Sprinkle with pepperoni and remaining mozzarella. Bake until crust is browned, 10-15 minutes longer. Let stand 10 minutes; slice.

1 SLICE *548 cal., 34g fat (14g sat. fat), 68mg chol., 1135mg sod., 32g carb. (8g sugars, 4g fiber), 27g pro.*

Homemade pizza is perfect for getting family friends involved in the cooking."

PORK SPANISH RICE

SERVES 4
PREP: 20 MIN. BAKE: 20 MIN.

- 1 medium green pepper, chopped
- 1 small onion, chopped
- 2 Tbsp. butter
- 1 can (14½ oz.) diced tomatoes, drained
- 1 cup chicken broth
- ½ tsp. salt
- ¼ tsp. pepper
- 1¾ cups cubed cooked pork
- 1 cup uncooked instant rice
- Optional: Lime wedges and minced cilantro

In the Titan Pan, saute green pepper and onion in butter until tender. Stir in the tomatoes, broth, salt and pepper. Bring to a boil; stir in pork and rice.

Cover and bake at 350° until rice is tender and liquid is absorbed, 20-25 minutes. Stir before serving. If desired, serve with lime wedges and top with minced cilantro.

1 CUP *304 cal., 12g fat (6g sat. fat), 71mg chol., 756mg sod., 29g carb. (5g sugars, 3g fiber), 21g pro.*

MUGHALI CHICKEN

SERVES 6
TAKES: 30 MIN.

- 4 cardamom pods
- 10 garlic cloves, peeled
- 6 whole cloves
- 4½ tsp. chopped fresh gingerroot
- 1 Tbsp. unblanched almonds
- 1 Tbsp. salted cashews
- 1 tsp. ground cinnamon
- 6 small red onions, halved and sliced
- 4 jalapeno peppers, seeded and finely chopped
- ¼ cup canola oil
- 3 Tbsp. water
- 1½ lbs. boneless skinless chicken breasts, cut into ½-in. cubes
- 1 cup coconut milk
- 1 cup plain yogurt
- 1 tsp. ground turmeric
- Fresh cilantro leaves
- Hot cooked basmati rice, optional

Remove seeds from cardamom pods; place in a food processor. Add the garlic, cloves, ginger, almonds, cashews and cinnamon; cover and process until blended. Set aside.

In the Titan Pan, saute onions and jalapenos in oil until tender. Stir in water and the garlic mixture. Add the chicken, milk, yogurt and turmeric. Bring to a boil. Reduce heat; simmer, uncovered, until chicken juices run clear, 8-10 minutes. Sprinkle with cilantro. Serve with rice if desired.

1 CUP *367 cal., 23g fat (10g sat. fat), 68mg chol., 93mg sod., 14g carb. (5g sugars, 3g fiber), 27g pro.*

"Flesh, bones, skin, gizzards, hearts and everything in between. You can and should use the entire chicken (except feathers, of course). It's the chef's MacGyver."

ZESTY NEW ORLEANS SHRIMP

SERVES 4
PREP: 15 MIN. COOK: 25 MIN.

- 2 Tbsp. olive oil
- 1 small onion, chopped
- 1 celery rib, finely chopped
- 1 small green pepper, chopped
- 2 garlic cloves, minced
- 1 can (15 oz.) Italian tomato sauce
- 1 can (14½ oz.) no-salt-added diced tomatoes, undrained
- ½ cup water
- ½ tsp. Worcestershire sauce
- ⅛ to 1/4 tsp. cayenne pepper
- 1 lb. uncooked shrimp (31-40 per lb.), peeled and deveined
- 3 cups hot cooked brown rice

In the Titan Pan, heat oil over medium heat. Add onion, celery and pepper; cook and stir 5-7 minutes or until tender. Add garlic; cook 1 minute longer.

Stir in the tomato sauce, diced tomatoes, water, Worcestershire sauce and cayenne; bring to a boil. Reduce heat; simmer, uncovered, 10-15 minutes or until slightly thickened, stirring occasionally. Add shrimp; cook 2-4 minutes or until shrimp turn pink. Serve with rice.

1⅓ CUPS WITH ¾ CUP COOKED RICE *371 cal., 10g fat (2g sat. fat), 138mg chol., 720mg sod., 48g carb. (6g sugars, 6g fiber), 24g pro.*

HOW TO

PEEL & DEVEIN SHRIMP

Pull legs and first section of shell to one side. Continue pulling the shell up around the top and to the side. Pull off shell by tail if desired. • Remove black vein running down the back of the shrimp by making a shallow slit with a paring knife along the back. Rinse the shrimp under cold water to remove the vein.

TUSCAN PORTOBELLO STEW

SERVES 4

PREP: 20 MIN. COOK: 20 MIN.

- 2 large portobello mushrooms, coarsely chopped
- 1 medium onion, chopped
- 3 garlic cloves, minced
- 2 Tbsp. olive oil
- ½ cup white wine or vegetable broth
- 1 can (28 oz.) diced tomatoes, undrained
- 2 cups chopped fresh kale
- 1 bay leaf
- 1 tsp. dried thyme
- ½ tsp. dried basil
- ½ tsp. dried rosemary, crushed
- ¼ tsp. salt
- ¼ tsp. pepper
- 2 cans (15 oz. each) cannellini beans, rinsed and drained

In the Titan Pan, saute the mushrooms, onion and garlic in oil until tender. Add the wine. Bring to a boil; cook until liquid is reduced by half. Stir in the tomatoes, kale and seasonings. Bring to a boil. Reduce heat; cover and simmer for 8-10 minutes.

Add beans; heat through. Discard bay leaf.

1¼ CUPS *309 cal., 8g fat (1g sat. fat), 0 chol., 672mg sod., 46g carb. (9g sugars, 13g fiber), 12g pro.*

"With most soups and stews, they're even better the day after they're made."

CAULI-PARMESAN MASH

SERVES 6
TAKES: 30 MIN.

- 1 large head cauliflower (about 2½ lbs.), broken into florets
- 1 cup shredded Parmesan cheese, divided
- ⅓ cup heavy whipping cream or half-and-half cream
- 1 Tbsp. butter
- ½ tsp. pepper
- Minced fresh parsley, optional

Place 1 in. water and the cauliflower in the Titan Pan; bring to a boil over high heat. Cook, covered, until soft, 10-12 minutes. Drain.

Mash cauliflower to desired consistency. Stir in ½ cup cheese, cream, butter and pepper. Sprinkle with remaining cheese and, if desired, parsley.

⅔ CUP *154 cal., 11g fat (7g sat. fat), 33mg chol., 290mg sod., 8g carb. (3g sugars, 3g fiber), 8g pro.*

RICE PILAF WITH APPLES & RAISINS

SERVES 4

TAKES: 25 MIN.

- 2 Tbsp. olive oil
- 1 small onion, finely chopped
- 1 cup uncooked jasmine rice
- 1½ cups water
- ¼ cup chopped dried apples
- ¼ cup golden raisins
- 1 tsp. salt
- ¼ tsp. ground allspice
- ¼ tsp. ground cinnamon
- ¼ tsp. dried thyme
- ⅛ tsp. cayenne pepper

In the Titan Pan, heat oil over medium heat; saute onion until tender, 4-6 minutes. Add rice; cook and stir until lightly browned, 4-6 minutes.

Stir in remaining ingredients; bring to a boil. Reduce heat; simmer, covered, until liquid is absorbed and rice is tender, 15-20 minutes. Fluff with a fork.

¾ CUP *277 cal., 7g fat (1g sat. fat), 0 chol., 599mg sod., 50g carb. (9g sugars, 2g fiber), 4g pro.*

CRISPY POTATO & STUFFING PATTIES

SERVES 6
TAKES: 30 MIN.

- 2 large eggs, lightly beaten
- 2 Tbsp. finely chopped onion
- ¼ tsp. pepper
- 2 cups leftover mashed potatoes
- 2 cups leftover chopped cooked turkey
- 2 cups leftover stuffing
- 2 Tbsp. butter
- 2 Tbsp. canola oil
- Unsweetened applesauce, optional

In a large bowl, whisk eggs, onion and pepper. Stir in potatoes, turkey and stuffing.

In the Titan Pan, heat butter and oil over medium-high heat. Working in batches, drop potato mixture by ½ cupfuls into skillet; press to flatten slightly. Fry on each side until golden brown and heated through, 4-5 minutes. Drain on paper towels. If desired, serve with applesauce.

2 PATTIES *364 cal., 19g fat (6g sat. fat), 118mg chol., 628mg sod., 28g carb. (2g sugars, 2g fiber), 20g pro.*

THE LOWDOWN

ON LEFTOVERS

There's nothing like cooking up a full Thanksgiving feast for family and friends — and having plenty of leftovers for weeks to come. But how long is it safe to eat them?
Turkey: Three to four days in the fridge; three to four months in the freezer.
Mashed Potatoes: Five days in the fridge; up to a year in the freezer.
Stuffing: Four days in the fridge; up to a month in the freezer.

BRANDY-GLAZED CARROTS

SERVES 12

TAKES: 30 MIN.

- 3 lbs. fresh baby carrots
- ½ cup butter, cubed
- ½ cup honey
- ¼ cup brandy
- ¼ cup minced fresh parsley
- ½ tsp. salt
- ¼ tsp. pepper

In the Titan Pan, bring ½ in. water to a boil. Add carrots. Cover and cook for 5-9 minutes or until crisp-tender. Drain and set aside.

In the same skillet, cook butter and honey over medium heat until butter is melted. Remove from heat; stir in brandy. Bring to a boil; cook until liquid is reduced to about ½ cup. Add the carrots, parsley, salt and pepper; heat through.

¾ CUP *153 cal., 8g fat (5g sat. fat), 20mg chol., 242mg sod., 21g carb. (17g sugars, 2g fiber), 1g pro.*

FAMILY-FAVORITE BROWNED ONIONS

SERVES 8
PREP: 10 MIN. COOK: 45 MIN.

- 3 Tbsp. butter
- ⅓ cup packed brown sugar
- 1 Tbsp. lemon juice
- ¼ tsp. pepper
- 4 jars (15 oz. each) whole onions, drained

In the Titan Pan over medium heat, melt butter; stir in brown sugar, lemon juice and pepper. Cook and stir until sugar is dissolved, 1-2 minutes. Add onions. Reduce heat to medium-low; cook until deep golden brown, 45-50 minutes, stirring occasionally.

¼ CUP *135 cal., 4g fat (3g sat. fat), 11mg chol., 769mg sod., 23g carb. (18g sugars, 4g fiber), 1g pro.*

"From bread to meat to vegetables, browning is the key to flavor. It's caramelization — and it makes your food taste better."

ITALIAN HOLIDAY COOKIES

SERVES 30
PREP: 20 MIN. COOK: 5 MIN./BATCH

- 1 Tbsp. sugar
- 1 tsp. grated lemon zest
- 1 tsp. vanilla extract
- ½ tsp. salt
- 4 large eggs, room temperature
- 2½ cups all-purpose flour
- Oil for deep-fat frying
- 1 cup honey
- Candy sprinkles

In a bowl, combine sugar, lemon zest, vanilla and salt. Add eggs and 2 cups flour; mix well. Turn onto a floured surface and knead in remaining flour (dough will be soft). With a floured knife or scissors, cut into 20 pieces. With hands, roll each piece into a pencil shape. Cut pencils into ½-in. pieces.

In the Titan Pan, heat 1 in. oil to 350°. Fry pieces in batches for 2 minutes per side or until golden brown. Add and heat more oil if needed. Drain on paper towels. Place in a large bowl. Heat honey to boiling; pour over cookies and mix well. With a slotted spoon, spoon onto a serving platter; slowly mound into a tree shape if desired. Decorate with candy sprinkles. Cool completely.

6 COOKIES *108 cal., 4g fat (0 sat. fat), 25mg chol., 50mg sod., 18g carb. (10g sugars, 0 fiber), 2g pro.*

QUICK BANANAS FOSTER

SERVES 4
TAKES: 25 MIN.

- 1/3 cup butter, cubed
- 3/4 cup packed dark brown sugar
- 1/4 tsp. ground cinnamon
- 3 medium bananas
- 2 Tbsp. creme de cacao or banana liqueur
- 1/4 cup dark rum
- 2 cups vanilla ice cream

In the Titan Pan, melt butter over medium-low heat. Stir in brown sugar and cinnamon until combined. Cut each banana lengthwise and then widthwise into quarters; add to butter mixture. Cook, stirring gently, for 3-5 minutes or until glazed and slightly softened. Stir in creme de cacao; heat through.

Reduce heat to low; carefully add rum. With a long match or lighter, ignite the vapors. Leaving pan on the cooking surface, gently shake pan back and forth until the flames are completely extinguished. Serve over ice cream.

1 SERVING *567 cal., 23g fat (14g sat. fat), 70mg chol., 224mg sod., 80g carb. (72g sugars, 2g fiber), 3g pro.*

DECADENT CHOCOLATE CREPE CAKE

SERVES 8

PREP: 1 HOUR + CHILLING. COOK: 1 HOUR + CHILLING

- ¾ cup unsalted butter, cubed
- 8 oz. bittersweet chocolate
- 6 large eggs
- 2½ cups whole milk
- 3 tsp. vanilla extract
- 1½ cups all-purpose flour
- ⅓ cup sugar
- ⅛ tsp. salt

WHITE CHOCOLATE BUTTERCREAM

- 8 large egg whites
- 2¼ cups sugar
- 1 tsp. cream of tartar
- 8 oz. white baking chocolate
- ½ cup heavy whipping cream
- 2 cups unsalted butter, softened
- 2 tsp. vanilla extract

SEMISWEET CHOCOLATE GANACHE

- 6 oz. semisweet chocolate
- ¾ cup heavy whipping cream
- 2½ tsp. corn syrup
- ⅛ tsp. salt

In the Titan Pan, melt butter and bittersweet chocolate; let cool. Whisk eggs, milk, vanilla and cooled chocolate. Combine flour, sugar and salt; add to egg mixture. Cover and chill 2 hours or overnight.

Place egg whites in a double boiler over simmering water; whisk in sugar and cream of tartar. Whisk until mixture reaches 120-130°. Stirring gently, keep at 120-130° for 2 minutes. Immediately transfer to a mixing bowl. Whisk on high speed 5 minutes. Reduce speed and beat until cool. Transfer to a large bowl.

Melt white chocolate with cream; let cool. Whisk butter and vanilla until fluffy. Beat in cooled white chocolate. With a spatula, stir a fourth of the meringue into butter mixture until no white streaks remain. Fold in remaining meringue. Cover and chill.

Lightly grease the Titan Pan and place over medium heat; spread 2 Tbsp. batter into pan to form an 8-in. circle. Cook until top appears dry, about 2 minutes; turn and cook 15-20 seconds. Remove to a wire rack. Repeat, greasing pan as needed. When cool, stack crepes with waxed paper between. Place a crepe on a cake plate. Spread with 3 Tbsp. buttercream. Repeat until 10 crepes are used. Chill 15 minutes. Repeat layering and chilling until 30 crepes are used, ending layers with a crepe. Chill.

For ganache, place chocolate in a bowl. Bring cream, corn syrup and salt just to a boil. Pour over chocolate; whisk until smooth. Cool, stirring occasionally, until ganache reaches a spreading consistency. Spread over outside of cake. Chill 1 hour before serving.

1 PIECE *781 cal., 56g fat (31g sat. fat), 179mg chol., 192mg sod., 66g carb. (53g sugars, 2g fiber), 10g pro.*

MERINGUE SNOWBALLS IN CUSTARD

SERVES 12

PREP: 5 MIN. COOK: 20 MIN. + CHILLING

- 4 large egg whites
- 4 large egg yolks plus 2 large eggs
- 1½ cups sugar, divided
- 1 Tbsp. cornstarch
- 6¼ cups whole milk, divided
- 2 tsp. vanilla extract, divided
- ½ tsp. cream of tartar
- Chopped glazed pecans, optional

Place egg whites in a large bowl; let stand at room temperature 30 minutes. In the Titan Pan, whisk egg yolks, eggs, 1 cup sugar and cornstarch; stir in 4 cups milk. Cook over medium-low heat 10-15 minutes or until mixture is thick enough to coat a metal spoon and a thermometer reads at least 160°, stirring constantly. Do not allow to boil. Remove from heat immediately. Strain through a fine-mesh strainer into a large bowl.

Place bowl in an ice-water bath. Stir occasionally for 5 minutes. Stir in 1½ tsp. vanilla. Press plastic wrap onto surface of custard. Refrigerate until cold, about 1 hour.

For snowballs, add cream of tartar to egg whites; beat on medium speed until foamy. Gradually add remaining sugar, 1 Tbsp. at a time, beating on high after each addition until sugar is dissolved. Stir in remaining vanilla. Continue beating until stiff glossy peaks form.

In the Titan Pan, bring remaining milk barely to a simmer over medium-low heat. Working in batches and using 2 soupspoons, drop meringue by ⅓ cupfuls into milk; poach meringues 4-6 minutes or until firm to the touch, turning once. Using a slotted spoon, remove meringues to paper towels to drain. Repeat with remaining meringue, making a total of 12 snowballs. (Discard remaining milk.) If desired, serve with pecans.

½ CUP SAUCE WITH 1 SNOWBALL *216 cal., 6g fat (3g sat. fat), 105mg chol., 88mg sod., 32g carb. (31g sugars, 0 fiber), 7g pro.*

NUTTY APPLE-GINGER CAKE

SERVES 16

PREP: 30 MIN. COOK: 35 MIN. + COOLING

- ¼ cup butter, cubed
- ½ cup chopped pecans
- ¼ cup packed brown sugar
- ¼ cup molasses
- 2 medium tart apples, peeled and thinly sliced

GINGERBREAD

- ½ cup butter, softened
- ½ cup sugar
- 1 large egg, room temperature
- 1 cup molasses
- 2½ cups all-purpose flour
- 1½ tsp. baking soda
- 1 tsp. ground ginger
- ½ tsp. salt
- ½ tsp. ground cloves
- 1 cup hot water
- Warmed applesauce, optional

Preheat oven to 350°. Place butter in the Titan Pan. Place in oven until butter is melted, 4-5 minutes; carefully swirl to coat evenly. Sprinkle with pecans and brown sugar; drizzle with molasses. Arrange apple slices in a single layer over sugar, cut side down.

In a large bowl, cream butter and sugar until light and fluffy, 5-7 minutes. Beat in egg, then molasses. In another bowl, whisk flour, baking soda, ginger, salt and cloves; gradually add to creamed mixture. Stir in hot water.

Pour over apples. Bake until a toothpick inserted in center comes out clean, 35-40 minutes. Cool 10 minutes before inverting onto a serving plate. Serve warm, with applesauce if desired.

1 SLICE *294 cal., 12g fat (6g sat. fat), 35mg chol., 276mg sod., 46g carb. (30g sugars, 1g fiber), 3g pro.*

"There is the belief that it takes 10,000 hours to become an expert at anything. That certainly holds true for cooking. Repetition turns good cooks into great ones."

Almond Berry Pancakes, p. 17

Flavorful Beef Flautas, p. 78

Tuscan Portobello Stew, p. 201

BREAKFAST

SMALL PLATES

MAIN COURSES

SIDES

DESSERTS

Crispy Potato & Stuffing Patties, p. 206

Sour Cream Peach Kuchen, p. 113